The Metaphysical Handbook

The Metaphysical Handbook

Laura Monahan

amazon kindle

Printed in the United States of America

Layout design by Arielle Axelrod

Cover design by Soofeeya Tamseel

ISBN: 978-1-7339215-1-0

This book is dedicated to

all those who have an inkling

that things are not all that they seem,

and yearn to learn more.

CONTENTS

Part Three
Relationships

Part Four

Manifestation

PREFACE

"Two roads diverged in a wood, and I, I took the road that is less traveled by, and that has made all the difference." - Robert Frost

I wrote this book because I was upset. After many years, I had attended a traditional church service, and was appalled to catch the man on stage telling half-truths. Everyone in the audience was eating it up. It felt very, very wrong. I didn't stand up that day, but I knew that I had to. I decided to find my own platform. I couldn't very well let everyone on Earth be taken by this man and the likes of him. First, I spoke at the Metaphysical Church I attended, and then, I decided to write this book.

The Metaphysical Handbook is designed to support awakening people. I needed a lot of support after I awakened, and I had to find it over many avenues. I spent years gathering this information. I was obsessed with it. My life gave me reason to. And now, instead of searching it all out as I did, you can find it in one, neat place.

My hope for you is that you evolve more quickly, and easily than I, thereby accelerating the rising consciousness of humanity and our planet. This book is a collection of tools, information, wisdom, and personal stories to empower and assist you in your ascension. Due to the scope of topics covered, some of these may be more pertinent to you at this time than others, in which case, feel free to move around the book as you feel drawn rather than reading it linearly.

I've made some really great choices, as well as some really great mistakes in my life. I've also spent a lot of time reading, contemplating, and practicing metaphysics. And now it is my intention that you receive all the good possible that came from this knowledge and these experiences. Then there will be no regrets, only lessons.

INTRODUCTION

To enter into the world of Metaphysics is to begin a life of wonder. You will see things that you do not normally see, hear things that you do not normally hear, and know things that will change the very color of your existence. As they say in Aladdin, it will open up a whole new world.

It was my awakening to this particular type of spirituality that has led me to believe that magic is indeed real. This journey has gifted me with all sorts of tools that have enhanced my life so much that sharing them has become more of a necessity and less of an option.

When I first became aware that life wasn't quite what it appeared to be, I decided to go on a quest, a quest for enlightenment. But there were clues that foreshadowed this. As a child, when people asked me what I wanted to do when I grew up, I would say that I wanted to be an adventurer. Little did I know, that adventure would be as much of an exploration of my inner world as of my outer world.

While many young adults were embarking out on careers and starting the beginnings of a family out of college, I was already on a different sort of search. My paradigm had been shifted so dramatically through my own awakening at 19, and then through my experiences in the Peace Corps that I no longer held the same aspirations as I did throughout high school and college. Immediately after my awakening, I was a different person. My life was then rocked by a series of "Aha moments," and it became my mission to seek out and experience more of them. Each one left me shaken, sometimes inspired, and feeling more awake than ever. Yet the world I was living in was transforming into an entirely different one. I began to feel a joy of a different sort, an even more refreshing one. Metaphysics were my oysters of truth, and I couldn't wait to pry open more.

The downside of this was while I was experiencing many positive emotions; there were also a gamut of negative ones. I have learned many Metaphysical techniques to restore my equanimity, and I share these here in this book.

As you embark on your own journey through what lies in the following pages, may your life too be filled with wonder, and may you experience that magic is indeed real.

In Love and Light,

Laura Monahan

PART ONE

MEDITATION AND AWARENESS TOOLS

"Most of us spend every waking moment lost in the movie of our lives. Until we see that an alternative to this enchantment exists, we are entirely at the mercy of appearances." -Sam Harris

Waking Up

If you haven't yet had an awakening to the unseen world, I would consider asking for one. My awakening was certainly a surprise to me. Though I had been praying for it for quite some time without understanding what I was asking for.

I grew up Catholic. So, as a child, what I consciously knew of spirituality was reciting prayers, comfortable ritual, and basically going through the motions. And I'm actually happy to have grown up like that. It was a lot of fun. Church, for me, meant playing games with my little brother and getting in trouble. I was forced to participate in seemingly meaningless ritual, and yet it was fertile ground for a future spiritual aspirant.

Then, in my junior year of high school, I met my first boyfriend, John. John was funny and loving. He was also Southern Baptist and had an entirely different set of beliefs than me, not that I had that many. While church for me meant goofing off or spacing out, he was passionate about what he called "having a personal relationship with Jesus." Initially, it sounded strange, only his enthusiasm was contagious, and I was hungry for something more than my newfound taste for teenage angst. Having an invisible friend with the power of

God seemed rather appealing to me. John also was fervent about praying from the heart instead of reciting verses, which really did feel more meaningful.

I tried it. I practiced what he taught, and I was happier and feeling more fulfilled. Genuine prayer works! Fancy that!

Since feeling less anxious lent validity to what he was saying, I kept on learning. Only I soon found out that there were some cracks in his faith. Baptists, you see, believe that the Bible is entirely literal, the true and the only word of God. Like any good aspiring Christian, I started reading it every night, trying to make sense of it. As I was reading, however, I could tell that not all of it was completely true, and this was unthinkable.

"How could there be holes in the Holy Bible?" I asked myself. The realization left me feeling quite conflicted. So, lying in bed at night, I started asking for the Truth, the Real Truth. Whatever it was, I wanted to know it because apparently, I hadn't found it in the Bible. This new religious world had shown me that there was more to life than meets the eye. It just hadn't revealed what there really was beyond our vision. And I was just not okay with living in the dark anymore.

I brought up this obvious discrepancy to John: saying that not everything in the Bible is true because there is a section about non-Christians being damned when they die. This makes no sense whatsoever for an all-loving God to do. We argued about this a couple of times, and needless to say, did not end up at the altar.

Although short-lived as a boyfriend, I will never forget him or what he shared with me about a more intimate form of spirituality. And, since although flawed, since I found security through it, I continued my involvement in Christian groups in college.

I enjoyed the groups somewhat, and made some really nice friends, but there was still that lingering feeling that just as with the Bible, there was much more to spirituality than my college groups were sharing. And I felt really confused.

Finally, when the best version of the truth that I was able to handle came out, it was in quite an astonishing way. I was in my final year of college and visiting my aunt and cousins in New England over the holidays. One evening, while we were out to dinner, they regaled me with stories about their amazing psychic friend, Sue. I had never been to a psychic before, and their stories about her ignited an unexpected fire in me. I vehemently asked if I could meet her, and even though I was flying out the next day, they set up an appointment with her in the morning.

That night, I woke up to a strange dream about her. I remember getting up and walking around the house in a dazed excitement. Looking back, it was as if that dream was my intuition telling me, "This is going to be big. This is going to change your life forever."

Sue arrived the next morning, and outwardly there was nothing special about her. She was an average looking, middle-aged lady. Almost immediately, she started talking. She said upon meeting me that she had done a body scan, and that the only part of me that needed healing was my knee. That was strange, I thought, because it was sore every so often, and it clicked. She offered to heal it for me, and I agreed. It involved a laying on of hands. I really didn't feel anything besides her hands, and I told her as much. Honestly, I felt a little silly with this stranger's hands on my knee. So, she cut the healing short, and moved on to her next gift, which blew me away.

Sue started describing spirit people that she could see plainly in front of her. They were showing her things that were meant as messages to me. And it soon became obvious as I listened that these spirit people were my grandparents who had passed away some years before. What shocked me was that their messages through her were things that she could not possibly have known. They were things that not even my living family knew about me. I was beyond amazed.

Turns out, they had a lot of advice for me, as well as some telling comments. I remember one image in particular. They showed Sue a stair I was climbing; energetically that is. And how right they have been there. I have climbed a LOT of stairs since then. And yet another comment that has haunted me since was from my super social grandmother. She said that I wasn't "socially ambitious." It was so true, and yet no one else had commented on it, and I strived to change that.

Anyway, to put it mildly, the whole experience rocked my world! You have probably already heard of mediums if you are reading this. But coming from a Catholic background, I had no idea that my loved ones were still around. To me, my grandparents and anyone else who had passed on was living in some faraway paradise called heaven, and maybe were checking in on me from above every now and then, but basically were doing their own thing.

Then, here was Sue, showing me, actually proving to me, that they were nearby, that they knew me, and that they really, really loved me. The truth meant more to me than I can say. And somewhere in the midst of our meeting I started sobbing.

At the end of the reading, I asked her how she came about all this information. There was so much more taking place here than described in the Bible, or in any other text I had read. She gave me a couple of authors to read, one of which was Sylvia Brown, who ended up being one of my first spiritual teachers.

As Sue left, I gave her a big thank you hug and kiss. And as I recall, that was her payment. Funnily enough, she looked as bewildered by my emotional reaction as I felt. I don't think she was expecting to have such an effect. I cried off and on for the rest of the day, and actually ended up missing my plane back.

But that was not all. That evening, on the next flight home, my knee was throbbing from where she'd touched it. It had never felt that way before, and I thought to myself, 'Maybe there is something to this

4

healing stuff after all.' This thought would later awaken me to a whole other Metaphysical study.

Arriving home, I naively assumed that when I explained what had happened to my family, they would be just as blown away as I had been, and then we'd all be exploring these new ideas together.

Only when I tried describing my experience to them, they listened politely, but were not at all affected! This was a blow because I knew I had just experienced something major, and they were usually supportive of important things. Their lack of support, however, was the beginning of a huge lesson: Regarding spirituality, people go at their own pace, and some experiences are meant for some, but not all.

I still tried to share it with my best friend though. I thought surely, she would understand. I told her the whole story, and then asked rhetorically, "Can you believe that this whole other world exists?...Isn't it incredible?" Only this time, I was not only met with skepticism, but also with answers from psychology textbooks. Luckily, none of this was enough to deter me from the new path that I had found myself on. I had had a major, major experience and no amount of cold rationale could make me forget the truth that had lit up inside of me...

It was confusing at first, and even a little painful, this gap in consciousness between myself and the people whom I loved the most. I've lost friends because of it, as I'm sure you have, if you've been on the path a little while. Only now I've gotten used to having a different belief system, and instead have set the intention to attract people and friends of a similar energy level.

Above all though, I feel very fortunate to be on Earth, mixed in with so much diversity; especially when it comes to beliefs. So, no matter how fervently I feel about something, I will always honor those who feel differently.

Looking back at this awakening, I realize my enthusiasm to meet Sue was my intuition pointing me down the trail towards enlightenment. And that day has certainly been one of the most pivotal of my life. It was how I woke up into a world that I would eventually call the Metaphysical. And this book is the story of what that I have learned along the way.

Meditation

"Out beyond ideas of wrongdoing and right doing, there is a field. I will meet you there." -Rumi

Following my experience with Sue, I started studying. The first book I read was by Sylvia Brown. It left me mesmerized by all the possibilities that I had never imagined before. I ended up devouring several other of her books and was left astonished with her views on spirituality and the afterlife.

As I explored further, I continued to fall on one major common theme: meditation is one of the most effective means of spiritual advancement. I tried it a little, and enjoyed it. Though I didn't commit to an actual meditation practice until the Peace Corps.

Joining the Peace Corps had been a lifelong dream of mine, and so I did so as early as I possibly could. I was only 20 when I was posted to Mauritania, West Africa as a Health Volunteer.

The beginning of life in the Peace Corps is spent getting to know the people and culture, designing projects, and basically reframing life. It is also a huge personal adjustment, and being the only foreigner in a village with initially very limited language skills, I had a lot of time for reflection and eventually meditation.

The inspiration for meditation started when on two separate occasions, I walked by the Peace Corps library in the capital, Nouakchott, and a book caught my eye. There was a benevolent man in a robe sitting on the cover and of course it was titled, "Meditation." Something about the book spoke to me somehow, so I decided to pick it up. I thought, 'What could it hurt? It's obviously not leaving me alone.' It's like it was waiting there for me.

I brought it back to my village and read it there, in the heat, surrounded by the mud walls of the room I was renting, and was immediately taken in by it. At first what got me most, were the reasons the author gave for why one *should* meditate. These were reasons that as an intensely academic High School student, I had been striving for, such as, an increased ability to concentrate, better memory, less anxiety, and last but not least, greater happiness.

I was also gently encouraged by the "how to" portion of the book. Meditation had always seemed like a very distant and strange thing to me. And yet, according to the author, all one had to do was mentally recite one of the prayers listed. I chose *The Prayer of St. Francis*. He's always been a favorite of mine. Then you just concentrate on every word without thinking of anything else for a half an hour. If any other thoughts come to mind, you start over. The simplicity of it, not to mention the promised side-effects, were more than enough motivation for me, and so sitting there in my remote village, I got to it.

I set about my new daily practice with gusto. Breakfast with my host family, Bikram Yoga or a run and then, meditation. Amazingly, it wasn't too long before some of the characteristics the author had described were coming to fruition. Slowly, almost without me even realizing it, I was becoming more relaxed, and having a little less anxiety. It was also becoming easier to get into a healthy workflow and live a productive village life.

The longer I meditated, the more my priorities shifted, and as I brightened, I became more confident. When I finally returned to the States, over two years later, I was vastly different than I had been right out of college. I believe that my experiences in Africa and the wisdom that stemmed from them made a huge difference, as did meditation.

Everyone didn't welcome my transformation though. Transitioning back into American life is always an interesting journey for the Returned Peace Corps Volunteer. For me, I had the added challenge of assimilating back into a family that was now dramatically different from me. For my parents, it seemed as though a stranger had come home to them, and they experienced even more dismay than when on a whim, I shaved my head in college.

Nonetheless, meditating helped me to maintain a pretty level head about it. I was also noticing a change in my awareness.

And so I stuck with it, and started exploring different ways of meditating. For instance, I learned that something as simple as breathing can be a meditation, and that contemplation is also a quite worthwhile form. And I found that the best place for me to do either is often in nature.

Time to Meditate

One of the other fun variables I learned to play with regarding meditation is *when* to meditate. I usually practice it in the morning when I first wake up because I've found that it starts the day off with peace and love. Leaving my meditation, I find myself in a more intuitive state than had I not bothered.

I especially noticed this improvement when I was working a 9-5. On those days I didn't feel like getting up extra early to meditate, so sometimes I skipped it. Only the days I skipped turned out to not be as smooth as the days when I did meditate, and so I kept at it.

Another great time to tune in is noon. I've found it is ideal if you're already feeling bogged down by the day to just have a refresher, which can also include a nap or some deep breathing if it's difficult to maintain a clear focus. These also can reset the mind.

The third best time to meditate, at least according to one of my spiritual teachers, is right before bed. She said that meditating 20 minutes before sleeping is powerful because it prepares a person for sleep. I think of it as an energetic cleanse, like brushing my teeth.

Another ideal time to get your meditation on is in the wee hours of the night. When you wake up alert and can't get back to sleep, then take that time to meditate. Part of the reason it's such a great window of time is that there is very little interference when everyone else around is asleep. I also read a study that between 3 and 4 AM the most DMT or Dimethyltryptamine, aka the Spirit Molecule, is released in the brain. This is the chemical that helps us to tune to dimensions that are normally quite invisible to us.

Finally, regardless of when you decide it's best for you to meditate, it also helps to keep doing it at the same time every day. This creates ritual, and there is great power in ritual. Imagine an energy vortex that forms when you sit down to meditate and grows ever more powerful each time. It is invisible, and yet, you'll find meditating in it is much more effective than a more sporadic approach to the upper dimensions.

Ideal Times to Meditate: Reboot, Reset, and Refresh

Time of Day	Bring Awareness To	Immediate and Measurable Benefits
In the morning, upon waking up	Intentions and type of momentum you want to create	Beginning on point gets that good energy rolling first and foremost
Noon	Where your thoughts and energy are	This will help with feeling more awake. It's like a pick-me-up to your morning that will get your afternoon going on a similar frequency
Before sleep	Readying the Mind and Body for Stillness	Prepares the mind for sleep. Ushers in a positive sleep experience, i.e. happy dreams
As a refresher throughout the day	When you're "off"	Turning back on by tuning back in will help you create more "on" experiences
3-4 in the morning	New ideas and New forms of ESP	Helps you to sleep more peacefully. There is also room for the type of newness that comes through in an environment with less stimulation
At the same time everyday	The Importance of Ritual	It will strengthen the meditation for you

Transcendental Meditation

Recently I learned Transcendental Meditation, aka TM. Now with TM, It is recommended that you practice it 3 times a day in differing intervals. Unless of course you are sick, then you are free to do it all day!

I was curious about what it would be like to transcendentally meditate all day, and it wasn't long before I had the chance. Food poisoning. I believe from the calamari at a local resort. And it was a bad case. I threw up all night, and then lay in bed the next day, not able to keep anything down. Not wanting to dwell on my misery any longer than I already was, I practiced TM. It was very, very comforting. Instead of thinking about the illness, and possibly prolonging it, I was able to transcend it, and achieve the peace that had been missing in my stomach.

TM has been amazing for me. With this variety of meditation, I noticed a significant lightening of my energy that distinguished it from meditations I have tried before. When done effectively, you'll notice it brings a degree of peace and lightness to the energy field that wasn't there before.

I would compare it to a watermelon radish. From the outside, the watermelon radish looks similar to any other radish, dark with roots. Only when you cut it open, you will find the bright, radiant colors of a watermelon. So, it is with transcendental meditation. From the outside, it appears to be like any other learned form of meditation; you're sitting quietly, gently. On the inside though, incredibleness is taking place.

TM also has some unique concomitants. One day, during my first week of TM, my transcendental teacher warned me that animals would be very attracted to me during this practice. I thought that sounded cute, but I really didn't believe it would make that much of a difference,

Well that very evening, the cats in the house tried to sleep in my lap during the meditation; both of them, which they had never done before. And then that very same night when I sat down to meditate in the cow pasture where I was camping, several cows approached me. I continued sitting very still; trying to stick to the meditation, but I was nervous because some of them were bulls, and I had never been so close to a cow at pasture before. And then, to my surprise, one of them put her nose on my face! I was amazed! And as much as I'd like to credit my animal magnetism, I have to attribute her sudden burst of affection to the special energy that comes from Transcendental Meditation.

Connecting Exercises to Assist in Meditation

Even though I've had quite the time domestic animals trying to join me in my meditation, I haven't had quite as much luck with my domesticated humans. My partner has been a little hesitant to meditate with me because he believes that meditation leaves him ungrounded.

So I have taught him a grounding exercise that helps him to reenter the world more easily when we delve into meditating together. You might try it too. It keeps you grounded by anchoring the body's energy into the Earth and then bringing the Earth's light up through the energetic centers of your body or chakras.

A more detailed description of the visualization is to see a point of light from one of your chakras, any one of them, travelling down into the Earth, where it intercepts the center of the Earth's energy. And then it travels back up, up, up through the Earth, and into the energy running along your spine. Watch. As the Earth's energy enters each of your chakras, it will become a little brighter. Then once you start meditating, you will already be grounded through this connection to the Earth, and you'll come out of it a little steadier.

You can also join with the sun, the difference being you send your energy upwards and bring it down instead of vice versa. When you connect to both, it creates a closed circuit of energy within your body and the Earth and the Sun*. This will not only help you to stay grounded, but also energized.

*You can also do this with the Moon or a favorite star.

Energetic Connecting Exercise to Assist in Meditation

Ground your energy into the center of the Earth; sharing a bit of your energy with the Earth's center, and then taking some of the Earth's energy back up through your chakras.

Do the same thing with the Sun's energy. This is helpful to do before or during any meditation or spiritual work.

Unity Consciousness Grid

The previous link made between the Earth and the Sun not only energizes and grounds you, but it also allows your energy to be in a few places at once. This also helps bring your awareness to those locations. If you like this idea and want to take it to the next level, I recommend also joining your energy to the Unity Consciousness Grid.

The Unity Consciousness Grid is the energetic web surrounding the planet. It holds and records consciousness. Anytime something or someone shifts in awareness on the planet, the network shifts with them, similar to the aura of the body. Consciously joining your energy to the Unity Consciousness Grid essentially makes you more conscious. As the Earth expands, so do you expand with it, only even more intimately when connected. This gives you a link to the "100th monkey" connection. Thus, when a certain proportion of the Earth reaches another level of consciousness, by being directly connected to the Unity Consciousness Grid, you will be more likely to make that jump first.

The visualization to create that direct link is similar to the energy circuit you created before; only the key is to imagine shooting a piece of energy from one of your chakras up into the Unity Consciousness Grid, and then again bringing that energy down through the energy centers of your body.

Turning on the Light

Turning Source Energy on is one of the most important spiritual tools. I've found. You can use it in meditation and in life. The Source of all that is comes in an endless stream of energy. Tapping into it feels right and good. It happens naturally when people pray and meditate, which is why they're drawn to these practices. The prayer and meditation bond them with Source bringing inner security and much craved connection. The visualization at the end of this chapter to turn Source Light on also achieves this, *only instantly*.

There are many reasons to turn on the Light. First, while being connected to Source fuels you with spiritual energy, it also helps anyone you come into contact with. For example, say after turning it on, you go into a grocery store. Others there will benefit from your presence and the presence of Source you bring via osmosis. This sharing will in turn lift you up albeit sometimes unconsciously.

You can even program Source Energy for what you want more of in your life by intending that it shine with your daily flavor, or what-have-you. Some of my favorite types of energy are love, peace, joy, happiness, health, rejuvenation, and prosperity. And if you want to have a little fun, you can also try, puppy energy. Perhaps you'll notice a subtle difference immediately. It is soft and unconditionally loving. But anyway, feel free to experiment with what works for you. Simply intend Source to flow in in the way you believe will help you feel the best, and feel what a difference it makes.

Regardless of how you program it, however, once you're used to connecting in with Source your bond will feel just as important as the energy you draw in from the sun, or even food. Source Light will also keep you going all day long, in that you'll feel connected and loved. Please keep in mind though that the satisfaction you draw in will be of a more spiritual nature.

Turning on the Light

First, ask yourself, How do I turn an actual Light on? With a light switch? With a string? Decide on your preferred method.

Then, imagine turning on a light.

In response to the action in your mind, watch as the light from Source flows into the crown chakra, at the top of your head, in an endless bright white stream of energy.

Experimentally, try programming it to different types of energy, and notice how you feel.

When you feel drained, ask yourself, is my Light turned on?

Once you've been turning on the Light for a while, try gradually increasing the size of the fountain of Light flowing in.

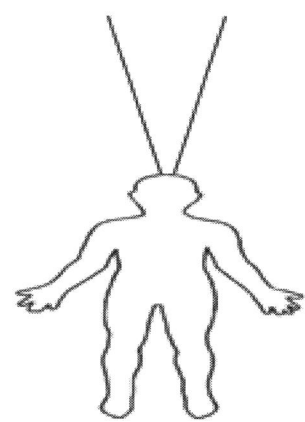

Connecting to Source as a
Relief from Addictions

As I mentioned, you won't feel as alone when you're tuned into Source, which makes it helpful in dealing with addictions. People overindulge in all sorts of things in order to achieve the fulfillment that a connection to Source brings. The 12-step programs like Alcoholics Anonymous and Narcotics Anonymous that are effective in treating their associated diseases work so well because they are spiritually based and tune a person into Source.

This gives people the feeling of Oneness that we all long for. Tapping into Source directly through Turning on the Light will also ease an addict's cravings. For myself, whenever I feel off, I ask if I have connected to Source yet? Very often, I have not.

Yet how does this happen? Well, when you turn on the Light, you are uniting Source as it exists outside, with the Source energy that exists within. It is all in your mind, almost like connecting two ends of a battery. You draw energy from the Source inside automatically, but when you connect to the Source outside as well, it magnifies the light and you feel even more of who you are.

I'm all for 12-step programs because I've seen the amazing things people have accomplished in their lives through participation in them. One of my girlfriends, Tara, was attending daily meetings for sex addiction, and she was explaining to me how she was even tempted at her meetings to have sex with the other people in there. Understandably so, I guess. I recommended that she turn on her Light every day and explained its importance. She felt the truth of what I was sharing with her, and now she not only no longer needs to go to 12-step meetings all the time, she is also in a stable, healthy relationship.

I recommend that you too turn on the Light every morning, especially if you are dealing with an addiction.

Mindfulness

I was recently in the little town of La Ventana, in Southern Baja California, on a kite boarding vacation with my boyfriend. And there I learned a thing or two about mindfulness: the art of keeping one's mind clean.

Mindfulness I've found, is in great company with meditation because while meditation quiets the mind from negative thoughts, mindfulness keeps it that way.

The first Mindfulness technique I learned was from Meredith Hooke, owner of ZenSmarts. Meredith had a meditation class outside her beachside RV every Sunday, which was so full of wisdom and zeal that everyone kept coming back. The huge tarp that she had outside for people to gather on was always overflowing.

That first day of the class was kismet. She taught us to monitor our thoughts through three simple identifiers, and she even had summarized them on a mindfulness bracelet that she gave to each of us as a physical reminder of the lesson.

The bracelet had 3 simple instructions printed on it that one can turn to whenever they have a negative thought circling through their mind. They are:

1. *Label it*
2. *Is It Useful?*
3. *Breathe*

In other words, first ask yourself, 'What type of thought am I thinking?' Then, 'Is it actually helping me? And thirdly, breathe through it.

I've found that this technique is super effective because once you label a thought it becomes less personalized. For instance, say you keep asking yourself, 'Am I a lesbian?' You would label this thought in your lesbian thought set. And if it is not useful to go through that thought process at the time because you're at work or something, then you would put it aside, take a breath, and move on.

Sometimes we have repetitive thoughts that go on and on and on, so recognizing when they aren't actually serving you for your given purpose in the moment, will help you to let go of them more easily, and move on to something else. Then, finally, there's the breathing, which re-oxygenates the brain, calms the mind, and helps to reset you towards a new line of thinking better fit for the moment.

This system of self-inquiry is also useful because it takes you out of the role of the thinker, and into the role of the observer. When you're the observer, it is much easier to let go and move on. You will find you can literally jump out of the negative thought spiral, and into a new, uplifting one.

The second mindfulness technique I found within a few weeks (Was the Universe ever delivering or what?) comes from the book, *The Monk Who Sold His Ferrari* by Robin S. Sharma that my boyfriend and I were reading on the trip. The monk in the story teaches his student how to use worry beads: whenever he thinks an unhelpful thought, he detaches one of the beads from the necklace he wears and puts it into a jar. Then, with the thought energetically wrapped up in the bead, he chooses a new, better feeling one to fill in "the space" in his mind.

I actually didn't have a chain of detaching beads to wear in Mexico, although I looked for one, so the way I had this technique work for me was by doing it in my mind. All you do is visualize the beads and the jar, and then put a bead in your mind's jar for every worrying thought. The last step: replace it with a positive one.

So, try doing this now...

No, really, try!

Okay. Your new thought might feel strange; like a flower in a barren wasteland. Only keep at it! New thoughts will bloom to attend it, and your mind will reforest itself again, only this time in beauty. Robin Sharma's bead visualization is like a cosmic reset button every time.

Side note-You may try assigning beads different colors for certain types of thoughts to help you to identify the themes and devalue outrageous thoughts.

When you think about it, it is painful to be on a worrying wavelength, so why not be mindful? Only, if you need another reason to de-clutter your mind, remember you can only keep so many ideas in your short-term memory at once, and some will serve you better than others.

Also, if a thought stays in your short-term memory long enough, it will transition into your long-term memory. And having too many negative experiences or ideas in your long-term memory is not good for your brain or your health. You'll be much better off if when something bad happens, to process it, learn from it, and move on. You don't want to keep cycling things through your brain, analyzing every part of them until they become something big and messy and then clog up your present-day life. This can prolong your pain and slow down your healing.

Instead, practice mindfulness, and create the life you truly want.

Mindfulness Techniques

1. *Go through the system of self-inquiry:*
    a. *Label it*
    b. *Is It Useful?*
    c. *Breathe*
2. *Visualize taking the negative thought out of your mind and into a jar, like the bead of a necklace, and replace it with a better one.*

When we reinstate ourselves as true masterminds, the gardens of our minds will flourish, and so will our lives. It takes a lot of reminding to get there though. I am still climbing that mountain.

PART TWO

HEALING

"Those who are healed become instruments of healing."

-A Course In Miracles

Energy Healing

Modern medicine does incredible things. Doctors and scientists are aware of many of the physical factors in health. Yet we still are not aware of the energetic causes of disease. Beyond the physical, why do diseases come about in the first place? What energies cause them? We already know that diet, exercise, and stress play a huge role in health, only why do people still choose otherwise?

Once these initial questions are answered, we can do more to prevent diseases before they manifest, instead of just treating them when they appear in the physical. Dis-ease first occurs energetically, and then physically, so when we're looking at disease prevention and treatment, wouldn't it benefit everyone to address its spiritual and mental contributors first.

In this section I'd like to share with you how I was introduced to energy work and then the different exercises that have worked for me. During my awakening with the psychic-medium, Sue, something was ignited in me that there is more to energetic healing than meets the eye. I could tell that she had had an effect on my knee the evening of the day she placed her hands on it by the strange sensation I had there on the airplane.

A few years later, when I came back from the Peace Corps, I decided to explore energy healing a bit further. I asked around at the New

Age gift shop where I was working for an energy healer, and was directed to Donna, an older woman with a kind heart, who would soon become my mentor and friend.

Donna had a healing practice in Jacksonville Beach, and one sunny afternoon she agreed to do a form of Pranic Crystal Healing on me. This was new to me, but I was excited for the experience. Unusually enough, before she did the healing, she let me know that she was also psychic, and so she may have some messages. I let her know I was open to that as well.

I lay calmly on her massage table while she moved a crystal over my body without ever actually touching me. Every now and then, she would gesture it towards a bowl of saltwater in the corner. Soon I was actually feeling things shift in my energy field and was getting more and more relaxed.

About three quarters of the way through the healing, she started talking about the pregnancy I had lost while serving in the Peace Corps. I was a little surprised because it was something I kept close to my heart, only sharing the ectopic pregnancy I had had with family and a close friend. Yet she cut to the core of it, and what she said affected me deeply.

Shortly after, something inside me broke. I hadn't ever really let the grief I had felt over losing the life I had held inside come to the surface. After the surgery, I had shifted my focus onto healing my body, and then once again into being a kind and helpful volunteer. Part of what broke was the gate I had shut on my hurt. So almost a year later, I found myself sobbing uncontrollably on a massage table with a near perfect stranger.

I calmed down eventually, and when she finished the healing, she explained that I'd either have a lot of energy when I got back to my house or be very tired. I left for home spritely enough considering, but when I got there I slept for hours, which is unusual for me even after a big cry. I realized when I woke up feeling like a new person that I had unconsciously been continuing the healing process. The Pranic Healing and the emotional release that occurred had worked their magic.

Learning Pranic Healing

Once I saw what a difference the Pranic Healing had made in my life, I decided to begin learning it firsthand. I took a few different classes all the way from LA to Orlando. And in summary, it is the process of cleaning unhelpful energy out of the chakras, and then replacing it with light from Source.

Now that I have learned it, I sometimes do Pranic Healing on myself. Recently, I fell off a horse. I really shouldn't have even gotten on that horse. Turns out, knowing very little about horses, and trying to impress someone is a recipe for disaster. My neck was really sore. I tried stretching. Nothing happened. Massage. Not much difference. Then, in my meditation, I had a vision that there was an energetic blockage in my neck, and that was what was causing the discomfort. So, I did Pranic Healing. It was immediately 70% better just from that.

The second stage of Pranic Healing, replacing the energy removed with light, I've found is very, very important because there were times when I didn't, and it did not work out for me. What I did instead was just to take the negative energy out in the shower, and let it go down the drain. I thought that that was enough.

Only to realize a little while later I felt no different from when I started. Turns out the chakras were just filling back up again with whatever, since I wasn't refilling them with the energy of my choosing. So that's why I didn't feel any better. The real reason for this is if we don't fill a void, then the universe will. And it will do so with the energy that we attract.

Taking out the bad and putting in the good is the basic recipe for Pranic Healing. However, the full Pranic Healing techniques are best learned under an official Pranic Healing instructor.

Reiki

Reiki is another modality of healing that I've found to be very effective. It is better known than Pranic Healing, yet very similar, as it can also easily be done on one's self and involves channeling energy. As with Pranic Healing, the healer sets an intention to heal and then charges whom they are healing by channeling Light from Source. They also channel the Light through their crown chakra and out through their hands. The only major difference between the two is that Pranic Healing cleans out the chakras before fueling them, while Reiki simply fuels. Nevertheless, much goes on behind the scenes in both, and miracles do occur.

I believe that anyone has the ability to channel energy, and therefore anyone can be a healer. How much energy they channel though, is up to how clear their energy channels are, and what "wattage" their body can handle. I recommend starting small and gradually increasing the amount of light channeled similar to how you would with an exercise program.

Regardless of which healing modality you choose, a little faith goes a long way. Just allowing yourself an ounce of hope that maybe this will work for you, will greatly increase the possibility of healthy change.

Belief Systems

More often than not, healthy change takes aligning belief systems. Beliefs play a huge role in how much faith people have, which can sometimes influence how effective alternative healings can be. So in any modality, examine your belief systems carefully. Delve deeply into your subconscious mind through meditation, dream work, hypnosis, etc. and recognize which beliefs are inhibiting you. This takes work. It's like cutting open a pineapple though. It can be quite a bit of effort, only once you bring those deep-seated beliefs to your conscious mind, you release them for the untruths that they are, replace them with healthier truths, and taste the sweetness of true life.

Questions to ask during your belief-revealing meditations:

"What thoughts, beliefs, and emotions could have led up to this condition or situation?"
And
"Which beliefs aren't supporting me anymore?"

It is important to look closely, ask questions, and really be honest with yourself because these attitudes are sometimes buried deep. Be patient because they can come up slowly.

You may not only have interior views that are contrary to effective healing, but also have ulterior motives for continuing to have a disease. So, as you process, also ask yourself, "Is this disease serving me in anyway?"

When my dad was seriously ill, I don't believe in his heart of hearts he truly wanted to stay sick. It was tremendously debilitating, and he was spending almost all his energy treating his symptoms, going to and from appointments, etc.

However, the perks that came with being sick weren't exactly a great motivation to get better and go back to work either. He was receiving a lot of money from two different insurance plans that paid almost as much as his salary. If you'd asked him if he was staying sick for the benefits, he would have said you are crazy, and yet I can't help but think it might have made a little bit of a difference.

My father was a good, intelligent, and kind human being, but he didn't examine his subconscious closely. He was already losing his lung capacity, and fighting to live. Psychoanalyzing his choices and beliefs were not a top priority but maybe they should have been.

I also can't help but wish that he'd delved more deeply into alternative medicine. I know he was doing what he felt was right, treating the symptoms, replacing the lungs, and I didn't yet have the understanding to present these new ideas in a way in which he might have been more receptive. I just feel like if he had taken the time to examine his situation from many different angles, and with a more open mind, he might have treated it differently.

Really, in hindsight, his belief systems were just outdated to his condition. If he had had easy access to open-minded Psychologists and Counselors to discuss beliefs and expectations with him, *and* felt encouraged in this direction, I believe he would have been much better off,. So please, if you're in a similar situation, I encourage you to go deep!

My dad's goal was to make it to 60, and six months after his 60th birthday, he passed away.

Louise Hay has a fabulous book called "You Can Heal Your Life," in which she discusses deeper causes of disease. Her book says that certain types of thoughts correlate with certain dis-eases, and then gives affirmations to change those thought patterns. It is a brilliant study, and I highly recommend giving it a look over.

More than *anything* though, if you feel like your beliefs are preventing you from anything, ask that those mindsets be revealed, in meditation, or elsewhere, the Truth apparent, so that you can easily allow yourself to heal.

An Illustration of a Helpful Belief System

A great many positive beliefs have also been instilled on us, sometimes from an early age, and for many, one is a belief in angels. I feel like this credence has enabled me to have quite a few conscious encounters with them that I may not otherwise have had.

One such experience occurred when I was in the middle of receiving Reiki from a group of people. We had invoked angels to help with the Reiki session at the beginning of the healing, but I didn't expect to become aware of any direct contact.

So there I was, lying on the massage table with everybody around me. Some had their hands directly on me, and some just had them hovering in the air. Then I noticed feeling someone's hands in a region of my body where I normally would not be comfortable having anyone's hands. They were right around my crotch, just resting there.

Out of curiosity, I looked down to see whose hands were so close to this intimate part of me. Everyone's hands were elsewhere. No one even had their hands above that area. And yet, the feeling was still there. That's when I realized that what I was feeling, although it felt like physical hands, was made of energy higher than my physical eyes were able to see. I believe that those were the hands of an angel.

This was an amazing experience because although I had heard of angels being present at healings, I had never actually been physically aware of them. I took it as a miracle, and a sign that my senses were becoming more refined.

Reprogramming Beliefs

I have come across a technique in years past that reprograms one's beliefs. In this technique, you don't need to know what your unconscious beliefs are to change them. You only need draw your awareness to what is bothering you and pick a belief to re-imprint instead. For example, you could use something as general as, "I truly and deeply love myself," "I am willing to heal myself," or "I have faith in my body's capacity to heal."

Reprograming Beliefs Visualization

Start by choosing a program that you want to take precedence in your consciousness.

Imagine your consciousness as an energy bubble and expand it out, out, out; first to beyond your home, then past your city, your country, your continent, out to even beyond the planet; past the farthest planets and closest stars, way, way, way out, all the way to Source.

Then, once you are fully expanded and tapped into Source, imprint the new belief system into your consciousness by speaking very clearly aloud, or in your mind, your replacement belief.

The Reprogramming Beliefs Visualization is a simple, easy way to start changing your beliefs. You can also speak affirmations to change ideas about yourself that may be inhibiting your healing. Try telling yourself, "I am holy. I am worthy. I am blessed." These are all great affirmations* to enlighten all of those mixed up messages we got as kids from our parents and other adults who received similar programming from their parents. It is now time to break that cycle. We already know deep down that we are amazing, wondrous beings. Let's open up to the truth, and fully realize it.

*For more information, see the Affirmations chapter.

The Importance of Channeling

Source Energy for Healing

It is possible to channel your own energy when you heal, but it is also extremely detrimental. This is key to remember as you embark on your healing journey because Reiki and Pranic Healing use energy from Source. If you use your personal energy, you will deplete your life force, and you will end up like the healers you see in the movies, run down and exhausted. I learned this lesson the hard way.

It was mid-morning, and at the pre-school where I was working, I was watching the kids play outside when all of a sudden, a little boy slipped, fell, and was crying. My instinct was of course to pick him up and comfort him; only at this particular Montessori school, it wasn't acceptable to do that. They were trying to foster independence and help the kids to self-soothe. Although I didn't agree with that, I also didn't want to get fired, so I instead I did what I thought was the next best thing. I reached my arm towards him, and in my hurry to bring him ease; I shot a hot blast of my own energy into his energy field. Moments later, he was up and away, laughing and playing with his friends.

I, on the other hand, felt like I had been shot. All I wanted to do was lie down and rest, but being at work; I just stood there, slightly swaying and feeling desperately weak. All I could remember to do was draw energy from the sun to restore my equilibrium, which helped. Yet, I was amazed at what I had done. I had used my own energy when I could have just as easily channeled energy from Source, and I was paying the price.

From that point on, I always remember to draw in light from Source. And I recommend you do the same. Whether you are consciously sharing energy or not, make sure your light is turned on and draw your energy from there. You'll be able to bring in a lot more energy and you will feel amazing.

The Healing Ball of Light

The following visualization is a healing exercise for clearing unwanted energy from the chakras. The chakras are intimately connected with the body, so when they are cleaner, the body is healthier. The Healing Ball of Light Visualization is usually done in meditation.

It begins with cleaning the first three energy centers in the lower half of the spine, which are the basic, sex, and solar plexus chakras, colored red, orange, then yellow. You could spend many months on just these three because you want the energy to run freely and cleanly through them before you go on to the other chakras. Then, one by one, you can start adding your upper energy centers.

Although it is preferred to do this sitting, you can also do it lying down, so long as your back is straight.

Eventually, if you do this often enough, your chakras will be cleared. And you will not only be healed, but also in allowing more light in, you will be that much closer to becoming enlightened. This is because when energy runs freely all the way up and down the spine, the Kundalini energy will also be allowed to travel all the way up the spine. When this happens, it induces a state of Samadhi, or a temporary state of enlightenment. Although it is possible for the Kundalini to be released from the base of the spine and travel up to the crown chakras without clearing the rest of the chakras first, it is a very dangerous practice that can lead to serious illness, and I would stay away from anyone who offers it. Instead focus on clearing the energy body. This visualization is one way to do it safely.

Healing Ball of Light Visualization

Turn on your Light to Source. *

Begin with clearing the first three chakras (Root, Sexual, and Solar Plexus) before moving on to the next one in the heart. (This will take time; maybe months if done daily.)

Sit with your back straight, and go into meditation.

Imagine a ball of light on the root chakra, about the size of a tennis ball, and spin it; seeing it spinning out any negative energy. Let it spin there for just a little while, then bring in white light from the ball or from Source to replace it

Then move it up to the sexual chakra. See it spinning there too, once again, spinning out the old, and in with the new.

Then move up the Light to the solar plexus chakra, and spin and replace it again, before bringing it back down again.

Repeat running the energy up and down your spine until you intuitively feel like the session is finished.

You can choose to see the Light running either along the front or the back of the body, so long as it is near the spine.

*See the Turning on the Light chapter.

The One-Cell Fill

Now let's look at a technique that will rejuvenate and heal the body on a cellular level. The One-Cell technique does just that. When you first make the decision in the morning to Turn on the Light from Source, also imagine filling up just one cell out of your entire body with this energy. One cell might seem pretty small to start with, only in time that cell will multiply and those cells in turn will multiply, and soon you will have a whole crew of light-filled cells. Your body will be healthier and just that easily you will be running at a much higher frequency.

I practiced the One-Cell Fill the other night, and I promise you that I noticed a visible difference in my personal appearance when I looked in the mirror the next morning. I was already looking at a brighter, healthier person.

I also highly recommend the One-Cell Fill because having more cellular light raises your energy level, and raising your energy level is an important part of evolving. For instance, the higher your energy level is, the easier it will be to tune to higher dimensions. I mean, why run at 90 Hz when you can run at 1000 Hz? At 1000 Hz, life is going to be more exciting and interesting.

Nevertheless, the main thing to remember when you decide to raise your energy levels through any of these techniques is to do so a little at a time. Again, too much light entering the body at once can short-circuit it; similar to how too much electricity can blow a light bulb. The One-Cell Fill starts off slowly, which makes it not only effective, but also safe.

The One-Cell Fill

Turn on your Light from Source and imagine it filling one cell in your body.

That cell will multiply; leaving your body filled with much more light.

The Activation of Healthy DNA

The One-Cell Fill is a great way to start rejuvenating your body. However, there are further esoteric methods of rejuvenation. This next one is based on our DNA.

To understand the following technique, remember that our DNA is multi-dimensional, and therefore still contains the records of the DNA from all of our lives. We can access this to maintain our health, vitality and even change our physical appearance. (If you are on the fence about past lives, I strongly recommend a guided meditation, a hypnosis on your own or with someone you trust.)

To start the process of activating your DNA, pick something in your body that you would like in perfect health. For example, you may desire a better liver. Then go into meditation (This method is most effective in meditation because in a very deep state of consciousness different dimensions are more accessible to the conscious mind.) Set the intention to see or experience a time in this life or any life in which your liver's DNA was or will be the healthiest. Finally, activate that DNA in your current body by seeing it lit up in the present time or sensing it any other way you choose to imagine DNA activated in your current time/space that resonates with you. (I am using past and future tense because beyond these 3 dimensions, we are outside of time and can access the dimensions other times are located in.)*

Activating my DNA has worked for me in marvelous ways. For instance, there was a time when I wanted more strength in my body. So, I went into meditation, and saw my essence in a very strong young man's body. Then I focused on lighting up that DNA so that it is manifest in this life. So far, it has worked; I have indeed manifested a stronger body although I consciously held onto my femininity.

I use the term Lighting Up as a visual reflection of the activation. If you are not a visual person, try using a sound or any other sensual stimulation in your mind that creates the activation. Regardless of the method, intention is key.

Activating Healthy DNA

In Meditation, remember a body you lived in/will live in in which the area you are healing is in ideal condition. Then activate that dormant DNA in your current body.

*See the Time is Now and DNA chapter.

Expectations

Our expectations are also fundamental. So, expect what you want for your body. For instance, rather than worrying about aging and all that, choose to affirm that you are expecting your body to rejuvenate. You'll find that you will then follow through with actions that help your body to rejuvenate as well. When the expectations are in place, the ideas supporting them will flow freely.

To facilitate it further, you can even ask yourself, "Which actions help me to feel healthy and vibrant?" Since our feelings help create our being, they are important. For me, I go to yoga classes, swim, and jog in the forest or on the beach. I spend lots of time outdoors.

Follow through with which actions resonate with you though regarding your own healing. Then when you say to yourself that you are expecting rejuvenation, you'll know what to do. When you're doing the things that help you feel your best, as your cells regenerate, they will be replaced with healthier, happier ones.

The next and probably the most important thing that keeps us youthful and vibrant is love. As it is pure, positive energy, it seems to be the elixir for almost anything. I'm surprised that the alchemists who were failing to turn metal into gold didn't discover that the ingredient they were missing all along was love. The more you love, the more loving that you are, and the longer you are inclined to live. The more you fear or choose not to love, the lesser the quality of life.

Alien DNA?

There often comes a time in a woman's life when she decides whether it's time to accept the existence of UFOs. I think that mine came when I learned that every star of the billions of stars in the sky is actually a sun like ours.

I actually tried to describe this to an African guy when I was in the Peace Corps who had had very little education, and he did not believe me! That in and of its self is an example of how limiting our beliefs can be without prior exposure to an idea.

Only if every star out there is a sun, then who is to say that there aren't also planets orbiting around some of those suns? And wouldn't it be probable that there is also life on some those planets intelligent enough to travel through space and pay us a visit?

Then there is also the possibility that life doesn't even need a planet. Or perhaps doesn't even need to travel on ships, or even a body, but rather uses its own consciousness as a vehicle. If a species didn't need a body, and we weren't able to see them, then it could be difficult to prove that they exist.

Another way of looking at it is to also know that things exist at different frequencies. And if something exists at a frequency beyond the frequency spectrum by which our physical senses perceive, then we wouldn't be able to even sense them to prove their existence. This, therefore, creates another range of ideas of how alien life could exist, and not just light years away, but in front of our faces, and we would also have no idea.

Moreover, when we get into the possibility of billions of parallel realities, this also leans toward a gigantic energy of life and life forms of which most of us would have no idea.

Fortunately, our psychic senses operate at a higher frequency than our physical ones, so a person tuning up to those could get more of an inkling of what is truly out there than someone solely perceiving through their physical senses. It is fortunate then, in this day and age that we have tools like meditation that help us amp up our frequency. It is also quite wonderful that there are people who are willing to serve as a mouthpiece for these higher energies and channel some of their knowledge to those who are interested. Judging by the resonance of what some of these channels are saying; their information is valid. It's up to you, however, to see what resonates for you.

I personally have learned a lot from channels, including confirmations of ETs. They offer an incredible gift to our population because they are making it so that even people who are not interested in developing their extra-sensory perception can have easy access to their information and increase their awareness. Ideally, channeling will become more and more mainstream, so instead of people getting persecuted for acknowledging their very real experiences, such as seeing a UFO, the experiences will be embraced by the general public.

It is up to us as a population, however, to express to those whom we have chosen to lead us that we are open to other life forms in other places besides Earth, and we are not afraid. Then they will feel supported in allowing the information that has come through to be released. People may make a big deal of it when the government finally releases all the information it's been hiding regarding UFOs and extra-terrestrials. However, deep down I don't think they're going to be at all surprised. There are some things we just innately know.

And what if the reason we innately know this is that we actually have been seeded with Alien DNA as some believe? This could be how much of our physicality has come to be; the infusion of DNA from different beings. And could it explain why humans are so different than other beings on the planet?

45

Moreover, if you believe in past lives, then isn't it also possible that we have had lives on other planets,? And if all DNA is superimposed in other dimensions within our beingness because all time is now*, then wouldn't it be possible to have access to that alien DNA just as it is possible to access the records of our other human lives?

If you take this idea into consideration, then when we eventually "graduate" from Earth we could have lives in other places as well. And once again, if beyond 3d all time is simultaneous, then these lives can directly affect our existence in this life too, *if* we choose for it to. It doesn't take much imagination to imagine other existences, just intentionality.

I've done some research on the different possible Star-seed civilizations, and the ones that have come up the most for me are the Pleiadians and the Sirians. The Pleiadians are characterized as being full of love, and the Sirians are very intelligent. So, for example, during a period of my life when I felt that it was of utmost importance for me to be more self-loving, I focused my energies on activating more of my Pleiadian DNA. And it has made a huge difference in how I feel about myself. However, if, for example, you are working on shifting your mental capacities, you could activate the extreme intelligence of the Sirians.

Turning on our dormant DNA, including the ET bits is a brilliant means of rejuvenating the body. This DNA work can also be used to help heal others, which leads us into the Imagining Perfection Method.

For more information on this, please see the chapter Time is Now and DNA.

Imagining Perfection

Imagining Perfection is an amazing and simple way to heal. Let me tell you a story about how I inadvertently practiced this technique, and how it turned out for the best.

I ran into a young man at a party. He was an attractive elfish looking redheaded acquaintance. He was also going through a rough time with a recent divorce. I happened to be talking about Reiki when he approached, so he asked me to share some with him. I happily sat down behind him and set my hands on his shoulders. He relaxed, and I began.

Just like in any normal Reiki session, I ran energy from Source through my head, heart, and hands, and into his body. Then, inspired, probably by the compassion I felt for him, I did a couple of extra things, which turned out to be extremely effective. First, I imagined the vibration of love and peace all around him. I saw the love as a pink cloud of cotton candy-like energy enveloping him; and below the pink, I saw light-blue clouds of peaceful energy engulfing his body.* Then, still feeling like I wanted to do more, I imagined my crown chakra opening more than usual and I allowed even more light through. Let me tell you, the energy felt exquisite. Only that night, it still didn't feel like enough.

I started letting new ideas float into my mind, and a thought I had read about Jesus's method of healing came to me. What I had read was that when Jesus was healing, he saw the person he was restoring in their perfection. So, I thought, 'Well, it worked for Jesus...' and I closed my eyes and imagined this young man in his perfection. I saw him in a stronger body, with even brighter eyes, and an air of confidence. His entire being radiated health. I got really into the visualization. In fact, I was enjoying the vision so much, that it seemed he wasn't anything else. It felt profound; him so perfect, with love from Source, flowing through me. I had always enjoyed his company in the brief times that I'd previously spent with him, only now my heart was open wide, and I even felt like crying.

Not surprisingly, that night a strong bond of love was created between us. I was seeing the best in him, without ever having even really known him. In fact, an ex-boyfriend saw us that night and told me later he was extremely jealous.

I left town soon afterwards on an extended vacation, and didn't see the man for a while, but a couple of months later when a friend and I ran into him, neither one of us even recognized him at first. He had put on about 20 much-needed lbs., was much more handsome, and was walking with an air of confidence that I had only ever seen in my vision.

This spitting image of the man I had imagined, standing before me in the flesh, was all the validation I needed that what had happened that night was very real and very valid. I feel like he made a significant leap in his healing that night, which then shifted him over the next couple months. Without him even being consciously aware of it, I had helped him line up energetically with some incredibly beautiful aspects of himself.

The Imagining Perfection technique has been a keeper for my spiritual toolbox ever since.

*See the Cotton Candy chapter

Imagining Perfection

When a person receiving healing is in a receptive space, imagine them clearly in their perfection. Take some time to see and sense them in all their wonder and beauty clearly and in detail. Then let the results speak for themselves in the time to come.

Time is Now and DNA

To understand how it is possible and feasible to cherry-pick aspects of you from all of yourselves throughout time in the preceding two techniques: Activating Healthy DNA and Imagining Perfection, it would help to have an understanding of how all time can exist now.

This concept can be challenging to imagine at first because we're mostly playing in 3d, 4d, and 5d on Earth. However, in the upper dimensions, there is no time. It all exists now. Therefore, from a broader perspective, everything is happening simultaneously. Time is an illusion. The old adage, the present is all we have, is not kidding.

Allow me to elaborate further on the ideas of mining the DNA through visualization and intention by explaining the idea of the circle of time through a simple metaphor. First try looking at time as running in a circle (Einstein also has a theory on a space-time continuum.) Only here, imagine time circling like tracks on a cd, and each track is simply a different part of your life. Say there are many, many tracks on this cd; that all of your life exists on and to live or relive a different part of your life, you simply play a different part of a different track on the cd.

Now imagine that the larger part of you, the you that is present with you, yet observes you separately, also known as the Higher Self, is the DJ. And now you as the Higher Self, should you simultaneously step into that role, are looking down at a collection of CDs. Each cd represents a different lifetime. And it's all there, every moment you've ever had is on a cd, and every lifetime you've ever had is in your cd collection.

Doesn't it now seem more imaginable that all your lives can exist at the same time? And you can have access to all of them? Therefore although you usually choose to tune into just one moment in one life at a time, that doesn't mean that the other ones do not exist. Again, all you need to do to switch from life event to life event or from life to life is to bump to a different track or even a different cd.

Now let's take this metaphor a little deeper. Imagine that the circular track on the cd is mutable; almost like pottery on a wheel, in that if we think and feel differently about the music, then the music actually changes, and as it changes, the songs before and after that song also change because they are all connected in a circular line to the track. Again, because they are all joined along a curving energetic line, when one portion of the energy shifts, it cannot help but alter the rest of the music as well.

To translate this back into our lives, what we think and feel in the now has the power to change the past and the future. It is all energy after all, and energy is mutable, so as time moves in a circle, the present affects the "future," which then effects the "past." Just as the Buddha says, "The only constant in life is change."

Let's expand this idea by adding inter-dimensionality into the mix. There is a paradigm that every choice we make leads us into another dimension, and because we are constantly choosing, we are constantly shifting; literally jumping through billions of dimensions every second. The dimension we are shifting into depends on the vibration we are emitting, which is also changing because we are constantly expanding. The entirety of us cannot go back to the same state of being we were at before because the entirety of us contains everything that happened since that point as well. So when déjà vu happens, it is not an exact replica of what happened before.

The whole concept is a blessing really. New vibrations continually make us new people, so we are only evolving. How sweet is that? It can be a comfort to know whether we label our experiences as "good" or "bad" that we are always learning and growing from them. It's one of the reasons that we are here, to become an even greater, more expanded version of ourselves. It is as if the infinitely expanding painting that is our Soul is getting a little more colorful in every moment.

So, the fact that every choice you make creates a new life, even if they are small and gradual decisions, beautifully portrays the fact that it is never too late to start over. It is also a reflection of the power you have in your choice of thoughts. No matter what your circumstances, when you reach for new, happier, healthier thoughts, you also shift through the dimensions, and then like a hologram, your whole reality changes.

Bringing this back to a healing perspective; when you channel Source energy to someone, for example, through Reiki or Pranic Healing, you are in actuality providing them with the energy to shift into a brand new person. It is up to them to let it work its magic though, and if they do, it can help them lift into a reality in which their disease doesn't exist. When this happens, even if it's just for a moment, then there is the potentiality of eradicating the disease from their body permanently. This is also why laughter is so effective in healing and as a method of disease prevention. These shifts are how spontaneous healings take place.

Shifting from one reality to another is especially evident in people with Dissociative Identity Disorder. Although it is not common knowledge, we all have multiple personalities. The disorder results when they are disconnected in a person. As evidence of how we shift in between realities and become different people; there are studies of people who when they inhabit one personality, have a tumor, and, when they are in another, they do not. So why not use this knowledge to manifest our best and healthiest self by consciously shifting into higher, healthier versions of ourselves, or just shifting from an ill person to a healed person?

The Time is Now

Time moves in a circle, and the entire circle is in the now when you go into the upper dimensions. When the part of the circle we are living in changes, it affects the future and the past. This is how the previous healing practices are so effective.

Future

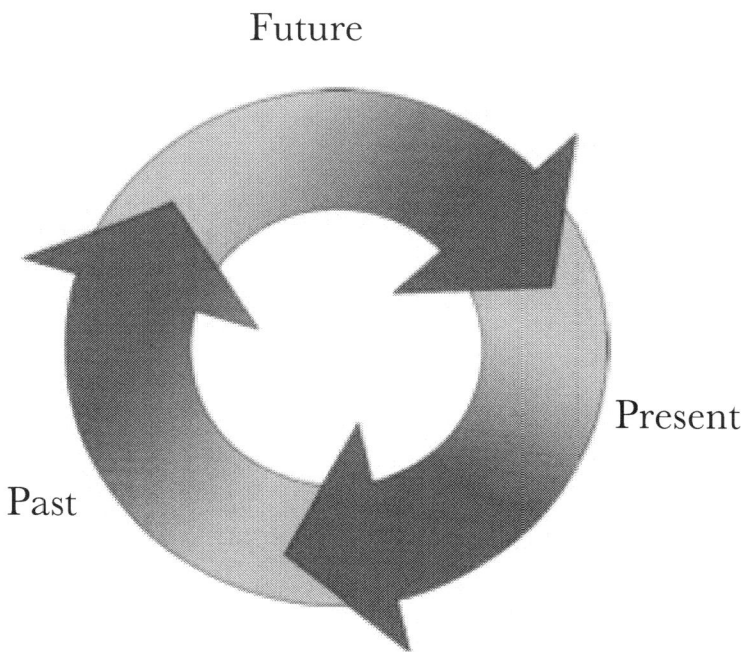

Past

Present

Picture on the Mirror

This insight into time and inter-dimensionality is also key to understanding this next method of healing because it too involves activating the different parts of your DNA that you would like to manifest in the Now. In the Picture on the Mirror Technique you bring forth different parts of yourself from this life to create your best current life. Using the cd metaphor, it is like you are mixing music between your life tracks so that your tune rings the most beautifully now.

This Technique does not even require much imagination! All it involves is putting up a picture of yourself when you were at your best, brightest, healthiest, your most vital, or youthful. The best place to put it is either on the bathroom or bedroom mirror, so that when you look in the mirror, your attention is also on that reality, not just solely on the present one.

Then, while focusing on this photo of your ideal self, say the words, "I am That, I am," or "That is me." ("I am," which is also one of the names of God, is a very powerful part of an affirmation.) Through the affirmations, you are bringing that track back into the current one playing.   Focusing on your perfections rather than your imperfections also amplifies them in your life.

This is a great practice for getting and staying healthy too, not to mention slowing down aging.

Picture on the Mirror Technique

Post a picture on your mirror of you at your healthiest, and when you look into the mirror say profoundly, "I am that I am" or "That is me" as you gaze at the picture and yourself.

Humming for Healing

The following healing techniques use the power of sound. The first, Humming for Healing, is quite simple and effective because it keeps the vibrations we create with the voice within the body, which then in turn refine the body's vibration.

One fundamental piece of understanding to this is knowing each of the major chakras correlates with a different pitch, and the physical location of the chakra on the body also relates to the pitch. In other words, the higher on the body the chakra is, the higher the pitch. So if you want to heal your third eye chakra as well as the physical manifestations that that chakra supports, then you would need to hum in the higher registers.

If you are unsure of exactly which chakra needs the most healing, and therefore of what register to hum in, try humming through the seven octaves, "Do, Ray, Me, Fa, So, La, Tea, Do." Give it a try right now. Is there a particular tone that feels the best to you? Then that is the frequency that is closest to what your body needs. I would recommend humming that pitch to your heart's content.

On the other hand, if you would prefer to hit a bunch of chakras at once and are not concerned with concentrating on a particular issue or area, try humming along with some music. It'll take you up and down your chakras, and you'll end up feel feeling more uplifted and upbeat.

But don't forget to hum with your mouth closed so that the vibration stays within the body and doesn't escape through the mouth. Humming for Healing is similar to what healers do when they place singing bowls on a person's chakras and gong them to make them vibrate. Their hope is that the chakra will resonate with the bowl's tone, shift, and become healthier. This is also a good idea, only Humming for Healing can be a lot more convenient.

Humming for Healing

Hum through the octaves, and when a particular tone resonates with you, continue to hum it.   This heals the body from the inside out.

The Hum-Ohm Technique

The Hum-Ohm Technique is also an amazing healing vocal exercise. It has the potential to be even more effective than Humming for Healing because much like Pranic Healing as compared to Reiki, it releases and replaces energy.

To take the first step, stand with your legs slightly apart, and put your hands in a prayer position in front of your heart. Tone the word, "Hum," and imagine any harmful energy is being released from your mouth; accompanying the sound. Then, turn your Light on and to fill in the void just created, tone, "Ohm" while imagining the Love and Light from Source filling you back up.

This is a great technique to do when you feel out of sorts because it gives immediate results. My favorite place to practice this is at the ocean. The Hum-Ohm Technique: a combination of sound, breathing, and visualization; is a formula for metaphysical success.

The Hum-Ohm Technique

Stand with your feet apart and hands in prayer position in front of your heart.

Turn on your Light if it's not already on.

Tone the word, "Hum" and imagine the stress or fear releasing from wherever you most need it to.

Then, tone the word, "Ohm" and imagine Light from Source coming in through your crown chakra and filling you back up.

The Whale Blowhole

This next technique helps release negativity in your chakras simply through visualization and the power of the breath.

Try The Whale Blowhole when you're out of sorts or aware of some stagnation in one of your chakras. I sometimes do it after my meditation. It is invigorating and works like a charm.

The Whale Blowhole

Make sure your Light to Source is turned on

Visualize a White Light on your basic chakra.

Take a very deep breath, and in one large, powerful exhale, release the breath!

As you do so, see the negative energy of that chakra releasing with the breath through the white light vortex you created as you exhale.

Reinvigorate the basic chakra with Energy from that vortex and also flowing in from Source.

Repeat the process with each chakra.

Six Ways to Prevent Disease

and Maintain Health

Before we go on with more metaphysical health techniques, I'd like to go into 6 very ordinary steps to foil illness and achieve good health. You probably have heard of these steps separately, however, it is rare to see them in a package form. They are not necessarily metaphysical, however, I want to cover them here for the sake of awareness.

The source of this information is Bashar the hybrid extra-terrestrial channeled by Darryl Anka. He is fascinating to listen to and has actually answered questions I've carried around for years. You may be surprised by how simple these six steps are: Oxygenation, Hydration, Exercise, Reducing Stress, Detoxification, and Lightening of the Diet, only the awareness of them has been helping me maintain my health and prevent disease for years now, so I would also like to present them to you here.

Also, already just in the treatment of cancer, many of these practices are recommended. I am not a professional health care practitioner; however, I can state from experience that these work. Please remember as you are reading that some of these may be easier for you to align with than others, and yet, they all need to be accounted for to create and maintain great health. Just begin with one at a time until you are comfortable balancing all 6 of them.

Oxygenation

I honestly hadn't thought much about this topic previously. I mean, we all just breathe. It seems so natural. It is only when we aren't able to breathe correctly, or when the air is so full of pollution that regular breathing is difficult that we take more notice of how important it is.

When my attention was finally drawn to this idea, I realized that I might choose a better location to live in terms of oxygenation, so I chose Hawaii as my next move where there are more plants, less pollution and therefore more oxygen in the air.

When I finally got here, I exited the airport, took a deep breath, and breathed the sweetest air I can ever remember. It was a complete change from the city air I had grown up with.

Not everyone wants to up and move to a virtual nature preserve though. So if you're like me, and you want to get more oxygen into your body without moving or becoming a frequent breather at an oxygen bar, try attending a yoga class where the deep breathing of pranayama is practiced. Or you could make an effort to keep plants in your home or office to oxygenate the air as you sleep and work. You might even consider leaving a door or a window open to let more fresh air in.

It would also be a great idea to set the intention to plant more trees in your area. Not only will this help clean up the ozone layer, but it will also bring more life-giving oxygen into your space on the Earth.

Hydration

Hydration is also of major importance for healthy living. It is a well-known fact that one's health suffers when they are dehydrated, and yet even with that motivation, it can still be challenging to drink more than enough water each day. I have learned that when a person gets thirsty, they are actually *already* dehydrated, so I've tried putting an alarm on my phone to get me back into the habit of drinking water every hour.

Only sometimes it gets boring to drink water day after day, so you have to come up with creative ways of making it taste better. I have soaked different fruits in water to make it better tasting. And I've heard in Europe, they have water fountains that produce sparkling water. Regardless of your methods though, I would recommend almost always having water around, so that you may drink as you breathe.

Exercise

Exercise is the third preventative measure for great health. For me, exercise has always been really easy to do. When I don't move enough, my body sends off distress signals to my mind that I need to expend some energy, and if I do not, this body feels very uncomfortable to be in. It has gotten so I can feel the energy building, waiting to spill out and be replaced with the fresh energy that comes after exercise. It's an early warning system really, and although uncomfortable at times, it has helped me exercise more than I ever would have.

I understand that not everyone has this system, nor if they do, are they always paying attention to it. Nonetheless, if we talk to our bodies, they will respond. Even if you don't feel like you're built this way, ask your body for some reminders, and it will work with you.

When you start exercising, a combination of cardio, strength training and stretching are best to ensure great health. So, I would alternate them in, and aim for exercising at least 2-3 times every week.

And if exercise is boring for you, (I'm not a fan of regular old gyms either) try new ways of staying fit until you find one that resonates with you. I love to run in nature, dance, or do yoga, but last summer for a change, I tried outrigger canoeing, and this year I'm doing CrossFit. Regardless of what you choose, however, exercise is super relaxing and reduces stress.

Reducing Stress

Reducing stress is the fourth and one of the most overlooked measures for great health. People generally avoid stress because it doesn't feel good, only they don't always perceive the relationship between illness and stress. And because they don't realize how harmful it is, they continue to live a stressful lifestyle for all sorts of reasons. In the long run though, it does not pay off. Eventually, and sooner rather than later, these people will get sick, and sometimes die prematurely.

In addition to changing your lifestyle, there are a variety of techniques that lessen stress. One of the first things to try when you start feeling that tightening in your body associated with stress is to take 10 deep breaths. The oxygen will relax you, and reduce the amount of the stress hormone, cortisol, in the brain. This is also the hormone affiliated with Alzheimer's, so the less of it, the better.

You might also consider taking 5, 10, 15 minutes out of your day to meditate or simply reflect.

As mentioned in the previous section, exercise is great at reducing stress because it releases a ton of good feeling hormones, and so does cuddling with our human and animal companions.

Anyway, explore what works for you, and relax.

Detoxification/Elimination

Detoxes are the fifth piece of the Good Health Puzzle. It is another looked over fact that our bodies absorb toxins from the air, water, as well as toxins from poisonous, processed, and conventional foods. Detoxes can get these out. Some people prefer fasting as a means of detoxing. I personally would rather go the herbal route. My favorite source is the American Botanical Pharmacy. It makes some powerful and effective detoxes. Additionally there are the ones at your local health food store, including many detox teas you might try. Notwithstanding, you will feel lighter on multiple planes after using them.

You might also consider sweating often, as another natural way to detox. The steam room and sauna, which many gyms and spas provide, are great for that.

Lightening the Diet

Eating more vibrant, local, organic foods is the last piece of these six steps.

I was able to lighten my diet considerably when I lived on an organic farm in Hawaii. In fact, the first week was like a detox, I was eating so purely. Only, you can also recreate these circumstances with a patio or yard garden. And if that isn't feasible, almost every city or town has a local produce market at least once a week.

Another easy tip for lightening the diet, especially if you're not into chewing up all those fruits and veggies one by one is to try juicing them or putting them into a smoothie. This makes it a little quicker and easier to eat lightly, and to get all those leafy greens, which help us to grow strong bones *and* stay emotionally, balanced.

I've also noticed that processed foods with chemicals mixed in generally help set people off emotionally, myself included. It is for this reason that I avoid them; only I had a week recently where I was feeling slightly off-balanced emotionally every day! I thought I was doing it all right, and was flabbergasted why I was emotionally off, and then I was reminded in my meditation that I had been eating a processed bar for my snack every day. So that was why I was losing my cool! Once I put those bars away, my temper evened out.

An idea to keep in mind when you are lightening the diet is that you are literally bringing more light into your diet. This is extremely important because of the little known fact that when you are eating, you are actually feeding yourself with the energy contained in the food, not just the matter; as most people commonly believe, and therefore eat for. This is why fresher foods are a more efficient way of feeding the body. They contain more light, and the body is better nourished because it is not just given ample matter, but ample light as well. It also explains why people don't need to eat as much when they consume a diet consisting of ample raw foods.

The structure of the diet program Weight Watchers illustrates this well. Weight Watchers uses a point system to help a person keep track of the quantities of foods they are eating. Most foods are assigned points and the person is only permitted to consume so many points per day. Instead of having to pay attention to the actual food they are taking in, all they have to do is count the points of that which they consume. The interesting part about this system though, is that most vegetables and some fruits are assigned 0 points, so a person can eat as many of them as they want during the day without jeopardizing the system. Thus, Weight Watchers is already encouraging a healthier way of eating through inadvertently rewarding people for eating light-filled foods.

I am not a Raw-Foodie myself. Only I do intend on eating lightly, and according to my cravings. Above all, I'm an "All things in moderation, including moderation," kind of girl, with an emphasis on energy and paying attention so that I know which foods help me feel the best.

The Six Steps that Create

A Dharma of Great Health

Oxygenation

Hydration

Exercise

Reducing Stress

Elimination/Detoxification

Lightening of the Diet

Intuition and Food

Even when you're aware that foods have energy levels, choosing what to eat can still be a challenge, but there are ways to make it easier. One is if you take a moment to reflect on how you will feel during, and after consuming your food. When you tune into your body, you'll intuitively know how good a food is for you. You might even try holding your possible nutritional choice to your solar plexus and tuning into your body then.

Of course, feelings notwithstanding, you might still choose to eat something you know is bad for you. I sometimes eat potato chips when they're right in front of me, and they don't do a lot for me. Believe me. Only when you do "slip up," try not to be critical of yourself because feeling good as you eat helps with processing the food. So intend on keeping those positive vibes going no matter what you put in your mouth.

Blessing Food

There is also the age-old tradition of blessing your meals before consuming them. This works because a blessing actually changes the energetic imprint of the food, and what was unhealthy before the blessing is healthier afterwards.

Try tasting your food before and after blessing it and see if you are able to taste a difference. Something in the blessing changes the resonance of the food, especially if that intent is a part of it.

A great one you can try from Kryon, channeled by Lee Carroll is:

"From my heart, to my heart, this foods resonates with my being, and nourishes it."

As you speak the words, bring your hand from your heart, around the food, and back to your heart again. Additionally this motion can serve as a symbol of your blessing if you don't speak or think the words.

You can also Reiki or share Source energy with the food, which also transforms and brightens it.

Local, Organic

Regardless of the blessing though, local, organic foods are known to be better for you. Organic foods are healthier because conventional foods are sometimes sprayed with poisons. And local produce is better than that that is shipped in because the magnetic energy fields of local foods are more compatible to the magnetic energy field of our bodies. Thus, if you eat what is already oriented with your energy field, the better alignment your body will have with the Earth, and the better you'll feel.

The Energetic Grids of Foods

And yet there is another way to transform foods into being more attuned with your body whether they are local and organic or not. Apply the following exercise when you are presented with nourishment that is not exactly what your body most needs in the moment, only it's all you have, and you're hungry. In which case, you can transform the food energetically into what your body needs.

To start to realize this idea, first you have to realize that there is an energetic grid around all food. Therefore, what you can do is if you don't like the energy of the food you're about to eat, you can just recreate a different energetic grid around your food in your mind's eye. For example, say you are craving protein and only have broccoli to snack on. All you do is imagine the grid of your favorite protein, and then place it around the broccoli. This will modify the energy of the broccoli into being more like that of a protein. You will then find that after eating you'll feel differently than if you just had the straight broccoli without any grid changes.

Also try this with liquids. In my hometown of Jacksonville, FL the public water is "cleaned" with chlorine and fluoride. The powers that be claim that they are helping people clean their teeth, which is ridiculous, because although they're teeth might be cleaner, in actuality they are hurting people's bodies and minds.

So, if you live in a city such as this one, don't hesitate to use the energetic grid technique with the water. Spring water is probably the best thing to transform it into because it is straight from the Earth. Not only is it pure, but it also holds the Earth's energy, which is very powerful and essential for our bodies. If you don't know what the energetic grid of spring water looks like, just imagine it. Intention is very powerful here.

Changing the Energetic Grids of Foods and Drinks

Visualize the energetic grid of the food or drink that you actually want.

Replace it in your mind around the food or drink that is not desired before consuming it.

Sun Water

Another great way to cleanse and energize your water is to harness the energy of the sun. It goes along the lines of lightening the diet because drinking Sun Water is drinking Light Water. The technique is similar to making Sun Tea if you've ever tried that:

I have a friend who jokingly calls this "Spirit Water." I love that he does because we are all on our way to becoming enlightened and raising the amount of light in our bodies will help with that. Drinking enlightened water is also a more efficient method of consumption because just as raw foods give us more energy because they contain more light; so too does Sun Water.

One question you might have is if we are feeding our bodies primarily with light and energy, then why don't we just lie in the sun and drink Sun Water all day to sustain ourselves? And the answer that may already be evident to some is that there are different types of energies, and our bodies need a variety of different types to keep them going. Therefore nearly everyone, except a few Masters in the Far East, need matter as well as light.

Nevertheless, if you're enthusiastic about losing weight for instance drinking Sun Water can lessen the need and desire to eat as much food, not to mention increasing your Light levels.

Sun Water

Leave a glass bottle of water in the sun for up to a couple of hours or more; depending on the sun's intensity.

Then, very simply, drink up that water.

(It is important to remember to leave the water in a glass bottle rather than a plastic one because the plastic will leak harmful chemicals into the water when left in the sun.)

Colored Sun Water

You can also use Sun Water to heal your body and to target more specific ailments by changing the frequency of the Sun allowed through the bottle. This is done through applying translucent color to the outside of your glass water bottle. I recommend cellophane. The colored cellophane will allow only light of that particular wavelength to come into the water through your bottle so when you drink it, your body and energy field are filled with that color. Different colors have different effects so you can start by choosing the ray of light you intuitively feel will most benefit your body. I would recommend doing some research into aura colors to see which ones you would like to be more prevalent in your energy field.

When I first started drinking colored sun water, I was going through a major breakup. And when I analyzed my feelings, I started realizing some parts of me were rather bent on destruction. Eventually I realized part of the reason for these tendencies was that I had a more than usual amount of red light in my aura. Now that's not to say that red rays are negative. Having a lot of the red ray can be extremely beneficial. It was certainly helping me to play better soccer and augmented my passionate nature.

Nevertheless, at this point in my life, it was also contributing to my distress. So since, I was still going through a lot of pain from the breakup, and wanted to rebuild, not just destroy, I felt that drinking more of the color blue (the relationship builder) would serve me better. And it did! Drinking blue sun water provided a bit of much needed balance for me, and it made a markedly peaceful difference in my life.

Experimenting with several different colors for your sun water to see what works for you can be a lot of fun. Another favorite color water of mine to drink is pink. After drinking pink water, I have felt drunk with love for people. I remember gushing over someone who was just an acquaintance while I was on the pink water. I felt a little bit silly about it afterwards only at the time it felt wonderful!

I also really liked the effect of drinking the violet ray. The first day I tried it, I was substitute teaching in a middle school geometry class, and I think I blew those kids out of the water with how enthusiastic I was about shapes and angles. The energy was obviously contagious because the kids seemed more enthusiastic than usual.

As you experiment though, keep in mind that different colors affect people in varying ways depending on how much of the color already exists in their aura, their sensitivity, etc.

Colored Sun Water

Wrap and secure the appropriate color of cellophane around your bottle.

Leave it in the sun for at least a half an hour and enjoy!

Masuru Emoto and Water

And yet sun and color are not the only ways to positively affect the quality of your water. You can use words, song, and symbols. The Japanese scientist, Masuru Emoto, did a series of experiments in which he proved just that. He published many of his findings in the book, *The Hidden Messages in Water*, in which he describes how he exposed water to different words, music, and images, flash- froze it, and then took pictures of the crystals formed.

And what he found was incredible! The water that had been exposed to the highest vibrational words, symbols, etc. also exhibited the most beautiful crystals. On the contrary, the water that had been subjected to more negative words and images, were essentially pictures of chaos.

Being that our bodies are mostly made up of water, one of the major takeaways people get from his work is to be very careful what you say to your body. If you want to raise its vibration, then choose high-energy words to speak to it, like "I love you" and "Thank you."

A fun exercise to experiment with yourself is to write a word of a frequency you are aspiring to on your water glass, or on the coaster that you put your glass on. I can vouch for the efficacy of this practice because when I leave my water on the word "Love" all night long, I swear it tastes sweeter in the morning. I also have a friend who has drawn sacred symbols all over his water jar and loves it. Allow yourself to be creative and experimental.

One thing that I also thought would be interesting to try along these lines is when a person is working to create a particular type of body for themselves that they leave an image of that ideal body on their water glass with the intention of reprogramming their cells to create this image within them.

Another idea is if a person wants to feel truly beautiful, why not drink water exposed to beautiful natural images, so that that energy is physically absorbed into the cells as well? I feel like there is room for many more discoveries to be made in this realm.

Sunbathing

This section wouldn't be complete without mentioning the healing power of sunbathing.

Of course, with the risk of sun damage, this is definitely something you need to set parameters for: sunscreen, sunglasses, etc. Only it bears mentioning because sunbathing is another age-old practice that draws Light in to heal the body.

So, one day, if you are not feeling your best, and it's sunny, try lying in the sun. Consciously absorb its life-giving rays and use the energy for healing and whatever other additional desires you have. For example, you might wish for increased brainpower, more understanding, or creativity.

This practice has been extremely effective for me. Often times when I'm on my moon cycle, I will lay with my tummy exposed to the sun, and this brings me additional comfort. It is the intuitive thing to do; healing and energizing. So, stop for at least a moment, and take the time to do what comes naturally.

Energy Protection

Protecting yourself energetically is key to good health and healing. We need protection in our day-to-day lives, so that we can be ourselves without fear of energetic repercussions, and also so that we can share energy freely without taking away from our own life force. You can harness and create protection with your energy through your intention.

Let me tell you of a time recently when I needed to pull in some of these protective methods. My boyfriend and I were living in a studio overlooking the ocean. He was away in San Diego, and I decided to go running on the beach at sunset with just the dogs.

I usually felt very safe doing this, but this evening it was nearly dark as I started back up the beach in the direction of the house. I was nearly halfway to the cliffs that I would climb to reach our home, when I noticed the dark shape of a man against the sea wall. His movements were jerky, and every now and then he would pick things up and throw them. People on the beach at this time were normally pretty relaxed; the kind who liked to stroll in nature, but something about this guy scared me. I doubled my pace towards home, and thought he would disappear, as I got closer. Instead, when I looked back a few minutes later, he appeared to be following me.

I looked around for the dogs. Buddha, my personal dog, was only a year old at the time. He was still with me; running confidently, but I wasn't feeling certain about his guard dog abilities. His mother, Camilla, on the other hand, who also liked to run with us, grew up on the streets, and had bitten multiple people for reasons unknown to me. She's not technically our dog but loves to hang out with us. She, however, at this pivotal moment, was nowhere to be found. And no other part of the pack that roamed our property had joined us this evening.

So, I was on my own without an official guard dog, and my fear started rising. I went through the exit routes in my mind. I had 2 ways up the cliff. An easy way, and a more difficult one that would entail some climbing skills; not something someone could easily do inebriated, which I assumed he was. I planned to take the more difficult one.

Then, to calm my fears, I started praying. First, I called on my Guardian Angel. The Catholic version that I was brought up with sprang easily to mind. It begins, "Guardian Angel, my guardian dear, to whom God's Love commits you here..." It's easy to remember, and speak in a calm, methodical, yet urgent tone.

Then I realized that my vibration must be slightly off to have attracted such a situation in the first place. So I said the protection affirmation, "I am safe and protected wherever I am," very confidently, and securely over and over again until I believed it. I've practiced this one, so it didn't take too long. Then I started feeling more confident that I would be able to make it up the hill before he did, and back into the safety of our gated ranch.

I looked back again, and realized I now had a larger lead on him. More hope. By the time I got to the cliff, he was way behind. I could make out his form; only it looked like he had turned away. Camilla, my unofficial security dog, also had finally turned up.

I started climbing; feeling relieved and wondering if I'd only imagined the danger when I saw the flash of an image in my mind. It was a cartoon turkey. Turkey, I associate with Thanksgiving, and Thanksgiving with Gratitude. I put it together. "Give Thanks." The powers that be really came through for me that evening. I was safe, and they were showing me that I had indeed received help in staying that way. "Thank you," I whispered

I wanted to share this story with you because although I was helped, I also had the knowledge to shift my vibration from fear to empowerment, which also helped. You can use these tools and tricks to keep yourself safe when you're not feeling that way either. You might be in danger. You might not be. Either way, it helps to dissolve the fear so you can think more clearly and get yourself somewhere where you at least *feel* safe.

Here are a couple things to remember. For one, if you feel uneasy about a situation, do your best to avoid it in the first place. This is because uneasiness is your intuition communicating with you. If I had seen that guy or felt that feeling before I started my run, I would definitely have done something else with my evening. However, sometimes I still find myself all of a sudden walking through that metaphorical dark alley alone, and then is the time to ask for help and clean up my vibration so that it is no longer fear based. Affirmations like "I am safe and protected wherever I am" work for me. Calling on my Guardian Angel also does. It's up to you, however, to decide what works for you; how do *you* feel safe?

Another trick I have is sometimes, I go out, and I don't want to be noticed, so I blend my energy like a chameleon. This is really just a matter of relaxing, pulling your energy in, and then imagining a sort of wallpaper around you that matches your surroundings, the true definition of a wallflower. It works very well for staying hidden, sometimes too well in that I've been in groups before and later people don't even remember seeing me.

I also have chosen a partner who not only stands 6'4, but also emits a very peaceful energy, and people generally do not mess with him. If they ever dared to, he would not engage, which gives us a generally harmonic energy when we're out together.

Moreover, I have put a protective crystal in the car for us, and I have other crystals that help protect our house. Therefore, our "dangerous situations" aren't usually as potentially dangerous as the one I was describing. When we do attract negativity from others, it is generally when he and I aren't getting along. For instance, once we were bickering on the phone, and someone hit him, and drove away. And yet another time, he got a ticket. A lowered vibration will attract these things.

Sometimes though it's simply a matter of protecting yourself from other people's bad vibes. Therefore, in this next section, there are some more protective methods that will keep your energy field strong and under wraps. This will in turn help you stay positive and peaceful while you're out and about in the world.

Psychic Self-Protection

Have you ever listened to someone's problems, and felt really uncomfortable? Yet, you didn't feel like you could just walk away.

Or have you ever had a conversation with someone and when it ended, you felt extremely tired?

Well, if you've answered yes to either of these questions, then chances are, you were the victim of a psychic vampire!

You see if you absorb someone's fears as your own after talking to them, then you probably absorbed their energy. And if you felt tired after interacting with someone, then they probably absorbed yours. Either way can be no fun.

Also, one of the major reasons that it's so important to protect our energy bodies is that when people drain your vital energy, and you allow it, they are inadvertently leading you closer and closer to death. Our vital energy isn't to be used to strangers we feel empathy with or family members causing drama, it is for our lives, and they are very precious. Even if you take on stuff that is not helpful to your health, you're still increasing the likelihood of passing sooner rather than later. You see how the Vampire myth isn't too far off.

The following techniques will help prevent these occurrences by limiting the amount of energy shared with those you're not comfortable with or those exhibiting destructive behavior. They're also good for just overall protection. These methods can be used separately or together.

Protection Techniques to Preserve your Energy

As you are interacting with someone whose energy isn't good:

1. *Imagine yourself as an open vessel, and see his or her energy going through you and into Mother Earth.*

2. *Recognize what part of your body is taking or losing most of the energy, for example, it could be the solar plexus. Close that part of your body off physically by crossing your arms or legs.*

3. *When you are done speaking with them, shake off their energy with some kind of physical motion that you find effective.*

4. *Limit the amount of time that you spend with these people.*

5. *Turn on the light from Source and let that everlasting energy flow through you to feed them rather than using your precious life energy.*

The Colander Protection Visualization

My one-stop shop, all-time favorite energetic protection procedure is called The Colander. I first started using this one when I was teaching in pre-schools. By mid-morning I was noticing that I felt completely exhausted. I would have to take the kids out on an early recess so that I could recharge in the sun. I knew that there was something fishy about feeling so drained because I am normally a very energetic person. However, I am also very empathetic, and I eventually realized I was absorbing the fears and other low energy emotions of teachers and such around me. Subconsciously I was trying to help them feel better by sharing my own energy and taking on theirs like I warned you about. It left me completely dwindled, and it was certainly not in my best interests.

Then, I learned the Colander Technique, and my days of desperate morning recesses were over. This technique hasn't just helped my work life. It's given me more freedom in all of my life. I can go out in crowds, and not feel tired or irritated. I can perform and feel rejuvenated rather than exhausted. And I can have heart to hearts with someone who is energy hungry and share without needing a nap afterwards. Let me tell you, if you are an extremely empathetic person, this is going to work wonders. It's a must have for people-people and introverts alike.

The wonder of this technique is that it only needs to be created once, and then you just zap it on every morning. And what makes this practice doubly awesome is that you neither take on other people's negativity, nor do they take on yours. You're only sharing Love and Light with one another.

Once you create yours, I would zap it on even before you leave the house because I've noticed a drop in energy when I forget. Try it on or off however and notice the difference for yourself

The Colander Shield

Visualize a large colander that encircles your entire energy body. (Remember your aura is large and egg-shaped.

Create it out of a type of metal, preferably either silver or gold because of its energetic properties.

Program the holes of your colander so that they only let Love and Light in and out of your energy body.

Zap it on everyday or whenever you feel the need.

The Eggshell Protection Method

Another super basic psychic self-protection method you can try is the Eggshell Protection Method. It's usually one of the first psychic protections learned. It is also perfect because it protects you as soon as you start a new day to help you maintain the purity of that day.

The Eggshell Protection, although it is still protective, is a little more porous than The Colander in my experience, so for me, I start my day at home, using the Eggshell Protection, and for things like going to work, I prefer The Colander Shield.

The Eggshell Protection Method

When you wake up in the morning, before you've even touched your feet to the floor, encase your aura in white light.

It should look very much like a very large white light egg.

Erasing Karma

Sometimes though, no matter how much we protect ourselves and keep up a high vibration, bad things do happen. And when they do, whether we like to admit it or not, it is usually a product of our karma. Yes, that dreaded word, the result of all our mistakes over lives and lives that we do not remember.

Now, however, that karma can be erased. And not a moment too soon!

I would have loved to teach my dad this when he was struck with his life threatening illness. Only then, I didn't know it was possible. At the time, his disease had seemed like a dead end; something we just had to put up with and make the best of. Now, however, if you're dealing with any degree of karma, it need not be dreaded or pined over any longer. You can erase it. Yes, like erasing pencil on paper. It is as simple as that.

I cannot stress how much this simple visualization will change your life, especially if you've been dealing with lots and lots of karma. All of a sudden, relationships will change; jobs will become different, family dynamics will simmer down... And you'll find your life is easier! Just one visualization, and it's all for the better.

If I knew exactly when I was going to take my last breath, right beforehand, I would erase my karma. Die free, and live even freer in the next incarnation...

Erasing Karma

Imagine a whiteboard, much like you would find in a classroom; the kind that teachers write on with dry-erase markers. On this board is written (fill in your name), "_____'s Karma." Now erase the board.

Instant Karma

You can also avoid a bit of drama if you erase your karma as soon as you feel some unease between you and another person.   I recently went on a road trip and inadvertently spent a little too much time with the girl whom I was traveling with. She was really annoying me, and I was starting to think some not so good thoughts about her. I'm sure she was thinking the same about me, and our friendship was showing for it.

Sensing the conflict, this would have been a perfect time to get out my whiteboard, and erase that karma, but I was too caught up in it. She ironically said to me the very things I had been thinking about her, and I was very hurt. This was instant karma. We ended the friendship somewhat abruptly, and I ended up flying home. I wish it hadn't ended so dramatically because it tainted the trip. However, you live, and you learn. And now I know that if I get myself into a similar situation and start to feel even a little bit of karma coming, I will erase it immediately.

I also recommend teaching this exercise to children so if they came into life with any karma, they can let go of it, and move on, without getting bogged down in the humdrum of it.

You may also wonder, why, if we've been dealing with karma for what seems like centuries and eons can we now all of a sudden erase it?

The channeled reason for this special consolation is that this a very special time in history for us. We're breaking free of the past, and the Creator has given us this concession. It's an opportunity to break out of this karmic cycle, and finally move on to other things. So, let's take advantage of it!

Long Distance Healing

Now that you've erased your karma and hopefully had a loved one do the same, it is a great time to learn about long distance healing. Because even without karma, a sick person may still be held into their belief system, and upon erasing their karma, they may get completely better or they may just not get any sicker. If your loved one is not close by and you want to help improve their health, try long distance healing. It helps to agree upon a time when to work on them. Reiki and Pranic Healing are both effective at a distance.

Here are a couple more distance healing techniques as well as the parameters that go with them.

Send 1000s Healing Angels

Sending angels to people during any time of healing or medical procedure is an effective long distance healing strategy. You can send them in lieu of worrying, and it will take a load off of your mind. You can even send them to strangers you hear about who are suffering if that brings you peace. It will help.

Keep in mind as well that there are also calming and comforting angels at hand to be used in helping reduce the suffering of the world. For example, if you hear of people in other countries struggling with some kind of catastrophe, you can send in the calming, comforting and healing angels. These are your psychic soldiers!

If this is your thing, please do not be shy about sending thousands of angels to whomever you think could use them because there are literally billions available. And remember to say, "Thank you."

Channeling Clear Neutral Light

You also might choose to channel energy to people whom you have heard have suffered a misfortune. If so, send them clear, unattached

Light from Source without any parameters to it. It is also of utmost importance to your own health that you don't send loving energy to those strangers, but rather simply clear unattached light.

It is tempting to send loving energy though. Believe me. Only this can also be a gateway to taking on their karma, so please just send the clear, unattached energy.

To sum it up, if you want to help someone from a distance, send them *clear* white light from Source and/or thousands of healing and/or calming comforting angels who know what is best to do with the energy. That way, they are helped, and you are free to move on without attachment.

Crystals

Along the lines of invisible beings helping us with our healings, as a metaphysician, you will find crystals to also be powerful helpers. There are a large variety of them, and each has its own distinct properties.

Here are a few examples of different crystals and how they may help you: Rose quartz helps individuals to love themselves unconditionally. Jade helps people to truly be themselves. And one of the major properties of diamonds is that it enhances love as well as lends protection. That being the case, what could be a better gift from a life partner than an engagement ring?

Another crystal that I particularly resonate with is Selenite, which brings peace. On my coast-to-coast road trip, we found an open mine of selenite out in the desert of Utah. We gathered up a bunch of it. It felt like finding gold. When I got back I circled my bedroom with it and experienced many an overnight chakra cleanse.

Nonetheless, if you'd like to find them out about a crystal you have for yourself, all you have to do is go into meditation and telepathically speak with it. Meditation is one of the most effective means of understanding your crystal because you will be more inclined to shift into the 6th dimension where they operate.

Once you know your crystals' particular inclinations, ask for it to manifest them for you, and keep it around to operate when it will. People often have crystals in their space by wearing them as jewelry. Only you can hold them in your pockets, and the effect they will have will be the same as if you were wearing them. I also recommend sleeping with certain crystals for comfort, peace, love, and protection. They can be a big surprise for sleeping partners who aren't familiar with that practice, but it's worth it. I had one boyfriend ask me, "What are all these rocks doing in the bed?"

It's also good to have certain ones around to decrease the amount of electromagnetic radiation from cell phones and other devices.

Crystals are amazing beings, and I highly recommend exploring life with them.

Mainstreaming Alternative Medicine

I've now described many of the holistic healing modalities that I am familiar with. Nonetheless, there are many effective healing methods that I have yet to experience. I mean the sky is the limit with all the things we can do to get ourselves back in order.

Still, it would be a lot easier to find and enjoy all the different homeopathic methods if they were a bit more mainstream. I mean I know they're more esoteric, but they deserve to be explored by scientists and the medical community without ridicule. Then, once their efficacy is proven, and they're opened up through all mainstream doctors, insurance companies, and personnel, people will be healthier and there will be less suffering in the world.

Additionally, if alternative medicine methods were more mainstream, and more people were given the opportunity to try them and see which ones work for themselves, their popularity will increase and there will be more money to be made. Now that is a win-win all around.

Another of the major reasons alternative medicine is so effective is that it focuses more on treating the cause of an illness rather than the more modern approach of treating the symptoms. As far as I know there is not a class in Medical School that explains how thoughts, emotions, and behaviors contribute to disease. Stress, I'm sure is covered, but the thoughts, beliefs, and patterns leading up to the stress? Just because science simply has yet to delve into it though does not mean it's not a valid path for people as we go about living our best lives.

I also find it ironic that so many herbs are processed for us in the form of medicine, or artificially recreated, and yet herbs in their natural state are not usually prescribed. Wouldn't that be a lot healthier? After all, nature is God's helper.

When my father was ill, he went to an acupuncturist, and she prescribed him herbs, only his doctors forbade him to use them because they were not aware of exactly what effect they would have combined with the vast assortment of medicines they were already prescribing him. This doesn't seem right to me.

The combination of natural herbs with other medicines is also worth some scientific research. Then people will have easier access to both, and more encouragement from professionals to go on a more natural route in their treatment plan. It's really up to us as the public to ask for this though.

Fortunately, some people are beginning to go in a more homeopathic direction on their own, and Reiki is proof. I recently heard that some hospital nurses were being allowed to heal using Reiki in addition to their other duties. This is a fantastic idea because Reiki is very soothing, which will decrease stress. Massage too, possibly combined with Reiki, would be health affirming in hospitals if it were prescribed as part of the treatment plan.

Eventually, as people become more aware, alternative healing will become a more popular part of our culture. One day an alternative medicine practitioner and a traditional physician will work hand in hand with a patient. People will have more and better options in front of them. We will get healthier quicker and stay that way.

Acupuncture

Acupuncture is one such modality that continues to grow in popularity. People simply cannot deny how they feel afterwards. It is also a treatment that works with the physical body to affect the energy body. The way it works is the acupuncturist inserts needles in the body, then energy runs between the needles, which helps the energy field. Since the energy field is affected before the body is by disease, when you assist the energy field, the body naturally follows.

My dad was more than a little skeptical of alternative medicine, but he was also in desperate straits. And as they say, desperate times call for desperate measures. He decided to try acupuncture as a supplement to his treatments on the recommendation of a relative, and he was amazed at the results. He said that he actually felt a wave of energy pass through him. That experience was all he needed to know that something magical was going on.

Looking back, the wave he felt was years of blocked energy finally flowing. I am grateful that he tried this because it may have earned him some more quality time in his body with us, and at least he felt better. Only, I wish he'd continued to venture into even more alternative therapies rather than relying so much on traditional medicine.

Emotional Freedom Technique, EFT

The Emotional Freedom Technique has brought many people a lot of peace, including myself. When I was going through my worst breakup, I was a virtual, literal mess, crying at nearly any thought of what had happened. Somehow that breakup brought up some issues with my inner child, and my feelings of loss related to my father's death a year before. My emotions reigned, and they weren't always healthy ones. Some compassionate individual recommended I learn the Emotional Freedom Technique, and I found it brought me a lot of relief. It would have been *much* more challenging to get through that loss without it.

After doing a lot of EFT, I've found that the reason that it works so well is because when we get right down into it, we all have regrets, negativity, etc. lodged in our energy fields, and letting those go is a huge part of our path to healing. The Emotional Freedom Technique or EFT gives us a head start on releasing some of these feelings and the issues that accompany them.

Another reason EFT is so effective is that it starts simply with loving you. It does so by bringing you back to those times that you may have deemed unforgivable. You allow yourself the space to feel the emotions surrounding those times, and then work up from there.

EFT works magic! If you want to practice it for yourself, use the following expression,

"Even though I (fill in the blank with whatever you did), I deeply and completely, love, accept, and forgive myself." This statement is rooted in self-love, and it works!

But that's not all it takes. While repeating this statement, you tap on specific energy points throughout the body. The tapping accompanied by repeating this statement shifts the frequency of the energy of the practitioner from one of negativity to one of Love. Sometimes the shift is gradual, but most of the time I've found it to be very dramatic, and always uplifting. In my experience though, it is always uplifting. Here is a brief summary of it.. However, more in depth versions of EFT that include the specific tapping points are available through You-Tube.

Emotional Freedom Technique, EFT

Start with the event that's giving you the most emotional pain, and briefly recount it to yourself.

Give the level of pain it is causing you a number from 1-10.

Tap at least 5 times on each of the major EFT points while stating:

"Even though I <u>the event</u>, I deeply and completely love, accept, and forgive myself."

Once you've tapped on all the points while repeating your statement, gauge your level of emotion again.

Repeat the process until you've reached a level you are more comfortable with.

Feel free to modify your statement after each session to fit your refining emotional needs.

Ceremony

One way to maximize a healing's power is to do it in ceremony. You can create a ceremony for anything for which you have a particular intention, and it will become more sacred and an even holier experience. Something as simple as cooking can be done in ceremony if you wish. I promise the food will be a whole lot better.

Ceremonies are effective because they include the heart and the directions. Honoring them helps create a sacred space. Whatever you feel great doing, a ceremony can help you make the most of that energy. It involves creating and sharing energy, which comes back to you in the form of your intention. You can do your ceremony through any medium, be it singing, painting, or loving. But I encourage you to look for the activity brings you the most joy and make into a ceremony. It's as simple as remembering what brought you the most joy as a child and trying it on again!

My preference is dancing. I set the timer, put some music on, and let loose. I didn't remember how much joy dancing brought me for a long time. Growing up, I just thought of it as something I had fun doing. Then, as I was looking back, I remembered that the times that I felt the most amazing was when I was dancing.

It is always a great idea to make an expression of gratitude during the ceremony because it will lift the energy. And you can even share the energy created in your ceremony with the plants, trees, the planet, and even the stars around you. They will send it back to you multiplied.

Once, before a big road trip across America, in order to receive more abundance during the journey, in ceremony, I scattered corn meal onto the Earth, as a gift to her while I danced. I got the idea from the Native Americans. Coincidentally, I ended up eating a lot of corn tortillas on that trip. ;)

There was also a woman missing recently on Maui. I couldn't help search, but I did pray and danced a couple dance ceremonies for her return. She was eventually found alive. And although I wasn't there, I felt like I had done my part.

Creating a Ceremony

To begin a ceremony, bow to the four directions; North, South, East, and West and then bring that energy into your heart.

Set your intention and begin your chosen activity.

To end the ceremony, bow to the 4 directions, and bring the energy back into your heart.

Healing the Earth

One of the best intentions we can have for our ceremonies is to help heal our Earth also known as Gaia. Because recently, Gaia has gone through a birthing process, a birthing of a New Earth into the fifth dimension, and she is still weak.

So often when I dance, I also intend the energy I generate to help her to heal as well as myself. I also recommend toning or singing to her and let the power of that vibration work its magic.

And people long to sing, more than we give ourselves credit for. It doesn't matter whether we were ever told we sing well or not because every voice has its individuality, every voice has its power. The importance of singing is really the spirit of the song and the love and the joy that we're expressing as we sing that is so good for our Earth and us.

For instance, I especially love singing in the car. And I take advantage of the energy I am creating through my voice by intending that my song be shared with the Earth. Only if you love to sing and want to share energy with her more formally, you could also do an actual song ceremony too.

There is an additional practice I would like to mention here for helping Gaia, and that is visualization. Instead of seeing her as we've created, imagine her as the Garden of Eden. And just like it helps a person when we see them in their perfection, so does she benefit from our visualizations. This practice also neutralizes the push and pull of light and dark energies, which in turn makes Earth a happier place to live. So, in a sense, we get healed together.

Since our bodies are made from her, she also understands what we're going through. Therefore, we are intimately connected to her. She too lives in a chosen consciousness that feels separated from the

Creator. She understands all too well that feeling of isolation we feel; the separateness we feel until we go within and/or reach out and realize we're not.

Because we are so intimately entwined with her, we often feel Gaia's emotions as our own. For example, there have been times when I've felt an emptiness that when I tuned into it, was not actually my own. It was of Gaia. So if you too have some inexplicable feelings at times, tune in. You may find the same source.

And you can help heal the loneliness by petting or rubbing her, just like you would with an animal or a friend. Go ahead. Try it. Or at least try to sit with her and see if you can feel out your own unique way of filling her up with love. Remember, whatever you do will also benefit you, maybe not immediately, but eventually.

One of my favorite ways of connecting to the Earth is to sleep with her when camping. All those moments of resting in such close contact are actually opportunities to relax and connect. A couple summers ago, I did just that while spending 6 weeks working on a friend's farm in Hawaii. She didn't have an actual room for me, so I slept on a mat on the ground outside. It ended up being such a gift. I would talk to Gaia as I got ready for bed. And walking barefoot on the grass to my mat, I felt her purity all around me. I would even put my hand out from my sleeping palette and caress her so that I went to sleep feeling united with her.

Finally, when I woke in the morning, I would inhale her sweet aroma and enjoy her energy. I would roll over and bathe in the cool dew. When I was doing this, I could feel her reacting to me. It was like she understood my need for connection and healing intentions. Even as physically small as my body is compared to hers, I felt like she was aware of me. It felt really good, like I was doing her and myself a great service.

The Dew Ceremony

Another way to cleanse and heal with the renewing energy of the Earth and the moon and star bathed water that she exudes every morning.

In ceremony we can actually program the dew to cleanse, heal, and even energize our chakras. All you do is when you get up in the morning, create a ceremony in the grass and rub the dew onto the parts of you that need it. I prefer to focus on the chakra centers, in the front and back of the body.

You might also like to focus on where your five senses are physically and spiritually located. For instance, try putting dew on your eyelids and then on your third eye with the intention of seeing more clearly.

Try as well to walk barefooted in your ceremony so that you're absorbing the energy of the dew through the energy centers at the bottom of your feet. This is a very special service you can do for yourself. Enjoy it!

Dew Ceremony

In the morning, when there is still dew on the grass, go into ceremony. *

Bless your body with the dew with intention and where you feel it will

most benefit you.

*See the Ceremony chapter.

Reintegrating Your Spirit

This next practice of healing will benefit nearly all adults. It came to me one morning when I woke up thinking about my family, and how I stand in it. Then I started reflecting on other families, and how although things in my own were far from perfect, growing up, I still had had it really good in comparison. The realization made me feel quite grateful for what I had.

Hindsight is 20/20 though, right? It is so easy to look back and see what went wrong, how my parents could have done better, how I could have done better. Only it is also possible, and perhaps a bit more useful to look back and grasp that I had so much to be grateful for too. Let's see...grew up in a gated community, I rode my bike everywhere, I took tennis lessons, I swam in the community pool, and ran around in the woods playing pretend with my friends. From that perspective, I really couldn't have asked for a more idyllic childhood.

And then I started comparing who I am now to who I was when I was a kid. I started asking myself: do I still have that spirit, that exuberant energy that I had then? I mean I was sort of wild. I would do all sorts of things that I don't do as much anymore, like pulling pranks, making wild jokes, building forts. I am a different person now.

And yet I miss that other little person, that wild, rambunctious little child. So, I asked myself, what is missing? What do I see in my past self that I and the all the other adults around me aren't exhibiting as much anymore? And the answer that I received, clear as a bell in my mind was: Spirit.

Somewhere along the line I've gotten disconnected with parts of my spirit. And yes, I've been gradually connecting back with it as I dance and sing, drum and play in the ocean as I'm sure you have too as you find different ways to connect with the Earth and your true self. And yet at the time, I felt like a part of it is still floating about in the ethers.

So, then I asked, what is the cause of this? How could part of my spirit be apart from me? Something I intuitively know is true. Did it get beaten out of me?

And that's when I had another Aha moment. Of course, it did. My parents were fans of corporal punishment, so whenever I did something, like accidentally hurt my brother while we were playing, which happened several times in childhood, they pulled out the belt.

It was painful and traumatic. And I tried hard to be good, but I was so mischievous, sometimes things got out of hand. I know now my parents didn't know any better. They were doing the best they could. It's what they learned from their parents, and they were born in a different energy than I was. Plus, there were 3 of us. I've realized this before, and I'd thought I'd worked through it. Only now was the realization that there were even further consequences.

So, I went back to my spirit, and regardless of what I'd already worked through, I still wanted it back in my body; quickening it, strengthening it, and loving it.

That was when I asked how do I reintegrate my spirit back into my body?

The answer I got used the power of intention, and the power of visualization. I lay down on my bed and saw a part my spirit as a blue ribbon of energy swirling around outside my body, and yet still connected to the rest of it inside. It felt very wild, so I reassured myself, 'It is my spirit and I am in command of it.' Then I saw it sinking back into my body, reattaching. It slid back into me on a very deep level, and I solidly connected it back in. I wanted it to stay put this time. I waited a moment. When I felt like it was fully reintegrated, I got up.

And boy, did I get up! There was an extra spring in my step and hope in my heart. I felt reinvigorated and upbeat. Something had healed within me, and I noticed another sort of change. Previous to that, I'd been avoiding my mom, and afterwards I was actually looking forward to texting her!

Going by that transformation there was some serious healing going on. Whatever damage she and my dad had done through their archaic methods of punishment had been significantly healed. I felt like a new woman and was looking forward to a new and improved relationship with my mom.

So, if you are not completely embracing our spirit, if you feel half-dead, like Frankenstein, including not wanting to get up in the morning, then try this technique. The changes may happen gradually, they may happen all at once. Regardless, it will help you feel more fully alive.

How to Reintegrate Your Spirit

While sitting or lying down, close your eyes, and see if part of your spirit is swirling outside your body.

Will it and watch it floating back into and reattaching with your body.

Then, if you feel like it, do a ceremony that reinforces this.

Harmony Visualization

As conscious humans of Earth, we want to feel connected and love for our planet. And yet it also helps to be in tune with the celestial bodies of which she is a part. Even though we may appear to be small in comparison with them, we are still an important part of this symphony. *And* we can move to be in harmony with the song they sing as they ebb and flow in concert with one another. All it takes is tuning our vibration to them. Then our thoughts, emotions and deeds will automatically fall into harmony as well.

You can achieve this through a simple visualization. You just get quiet and imagine the stars and planets around you as a symphony. Each one is playing its particular instrument, and all together, they are playing the most beautiful music. When you join in, tuning your little body, and synchronizing your energy to the orchestra; it moves fluidly with you and around you, and with pleasure.

Thus, the music of all these celestial bodies is actually enhanced by your contribution. And when you visualize and/or do this, your vibration shifts so that you are in tune with them. In a sense you become one with them. Your choices will then change to reflect your transformation, so that you're not only helping the world, but also the universe around you.

And that it is how to fall into harmony with the space all around you. It may seem like a small thing, but it can make a huge difference in your health, your life and the life all around you.

Harmony Visualization

Visualize the universe's planets, moons, and stars as all vibrating to individual frequencies that combined make a beautiful music.

Now add your frequency to the sound, and harmonize it with them.

Keeping the Home and Workplace Energetically Clean

It is also important of course to have harmony in the home. One of the cornerstones to healthy living is keeping the bodies we live in energetically clean. Only, what about the home in which our bodies live? And our workplaces where we often spend the most time? Isn't it important to our health to keep those up too?

Yes, yes, and yes. Just as people's energy bodies affect you as you interact with them, so does the energy of the environment you inhabit affect you as you live and work in it. "The Universe Loves Order," and the good news is when you keep your homes energetically clean through a few, simple tools, and your life will reflect the difference.

One of the most common ways is to burn sage. Native Americans have been using sage for centuries as an aura cleanse, only, it can also be used as a cleanse for the home. If you have a visit from any kind of unwanted visitor, that energy residue can be removed with a little help from your friend, Sage. Incense and Palo Santo also help raise the home's vibration.

And then you may also choose to transform your dwelling's energy through sound. At one of my friend's homes growing up, her father would always have country music playing in the bathroom. Even if you're not a fan of country, you've got to admit it has a high vibration, and their bathroom always felt wonderful to be in. My friend especially loved it. As a teenager, she would spend hours in the bathroom.

Toning too will raise a home's vibration. You can play recordings and/or tone yourself. My Pranic Healing teacher recommended playing an Ohm chant for a half hour after an argument to disintegrate the energetic debris left behind. Try doing this after any heated discussion, you will find your home's homeostasis restored, and it will be that much easier to start over.

Cleansing the Home's Energy

Sage

Incense

Palo Santo

Chanting, i.e. Ohm

Music

Cotton Candy

People take paint color and decor quite seriously because intuitively they know it affects their homes vibration. What is often overlooked however, is how you can consciously decorate your home or workplace with energy. The following tool is called The Cotton Candy Technique, and it does just that.

Have you ever shown up for work, bright and sunny, ready to have a great day, only to be shot down from your reverie because not everyone else was on the same page? That was often my experience working in pre-schools. I loved the children and I loved my coworkers. However, when they were processing things, I felt it too.

Which is why I started using this tool. It elevates the energy of the environment before anyone actually steps in the door, so instead of him or her affecting you, the environment affects everyone, and you are all much better off.

It starts with a simple visualization the night before. You just imagine the rooms filled to the brim with cotton candy energy. Choose the color of the vibration you want to manifest. Visualizing pink energy brings in Love. Light blue brings in peace. You can choose green, purple; yellow depending on the effect you would like to have on your home or work. Any color you're particularly attracted to when you think about the space is quite possibly the color that's best. Just use your intuition to decide which is best for your circumstances, and I guarantee you will have a much more peaceful, calm, centered day than you would have otherwise.

You can also Turn On the Light to your home or workplace. Remember the tool of Turning on the Light to your body. Well, you can do the same for buildings or any environment where you don't feel completely comfortable. Not only does Turning on the Light turn on this endless funnel of Love and Light, filling the space, it also helps

105

eliminate the competition for energy that sometimes exists between people because there will be an endless abundance of Light.

Cotton Candy Technique

The day or evening before you go into work, imagine a pink or light blue cloud of energy resembling cotton candy engulfing the entire workplace.

Life Energy

Another great tool for raising your environment's vibration is to have animals and living plants all around. They exude purity and consciousness that will bring life and love to your settings in a diversified way that contrasts with solely having humans around. You'll also find that not just you, but many of the members of your family and employees will interact with these things, even if it's not on a conscious level, which will in turn raise the vibration of the entire location solely through their way of being.

Some of the preschools I worked in for example, I witnessed firsthand that the plants and animals around were bringing major energetic benefits to the children. For example, have you ever noticed how much calmer a classroom is with the addition of a fish tank? The kids would watch that tank, and there would immediately be a calming change in their demeanor.

Different animals bring in different energetic benefits, as do different plants. For example, if I ran a nursing home, I may have a few birds around, and rather than cacti, I would have more perennials. But use your intuition to choose what's best for your environment.

Another often overlooked, yet powerful energy shifter for the home and work are crystals. Crystals bring in many different energetic benefits to the space, and body, so please pick the ones you most resonate with to bring into your space.

Basically, the more you can integrate the energy of the Earth into your environments, the better. And why not start at the foundational level of building? The architect, Frank Lloyd Wright was great at this. One paradigm-shifting idea similar to how he brought the Earth back into our environments is planting bamboo or another living plant that will double as a fence. Or, this Christmas, why not choose a living

Christmas tree that you can plant after the holidays instead of buying a dead one?

Salt Cleanses

Salt is used for cleansing so many things, including our spaces. A long time ago, when I was living in an apartment in Riverside in Jacksonville, I had a clairvoyant friend tell me she believed the problems I was having at the time were a result of the energy of the home. Her solution: spread salt all over the floor, leave it there 24 hours, and vacuum it up. Then change out the vacuum bag, so that all of that energy left with it. I was desperate, so I did what I was told, and that was the beginning of the upswing of that period for me. Later I met the previous tenant of that apartment, and when he described some of his experiences there, I knew my friend had been right. I'm, grateful for the process my friend taught me. However, it was a huge mess. I've since discovered an easier way of cleansing the home with salt.

This process is way easier than spreading salt all over the floor, and more effective. I've been doing it since I learned about it, and it has made a huge difference in my life and in the energy of the homes that I've lived in.

Home Salt Cleanse

Put a little bit of salt in a small disposable container (like a cap of a container that you would throw away anyway. (The amount of salt doesn't matter because it is not holding the negativity but grounding it). It has to have sides to it though; so it doesn't leak out.

Then program the salt with your mind so that it will channel all the negative energy of the home into the Earth, and seal it there.

When the salt is done working, you'll know it intuitively, although it can take days or weeks depending on the negativity. Then remove the container with your non-receiving hand because you do not want to receive any of the energy it has in it, dispose of it in the trash, and take out the trash.

Creating a Family and a Home

A person's health starts very early though, so as parents or parents to be, it is up to us to do what it takes to foster great health in our children. Through creating loved children who are raised in the healthiest way possible, everyone's future gets better.

In *The Ringing Cedars* series by Vladimir Megre, Anastasia, the wise and enlightened Siberian recluse, speaks to this. The following points are very important for anyone to be aware of.

The first is regarding preparing a home for a baby. Going beyond cleansing and cleaning, Anastasia advises consciously creating "A Space of Love" for your baby as you prepare for his or her arrival. Making nurseries, having showers, and acquiring all the necessary baby things is very common. I have never actually heard someone specifically say however, "We are making a Space of Love for our baby." And that is really what the baby needs, isn't it? Above and beyond diapers and clothes: A Space of Love.

Anastasia also addresses breast-feeding in a unique way that feels like vitally important knowledge. She says that while breast-feeding, it is best for mothers to concentrate their attention solely on their baby. The bond that forms between mother and child during breastfeeding is known to be significant, only, when women additionally remain locked in a gaze with their child and focus all their attention on the baby during the feedings, these women are transmitting much more than milk. They are also sharing a deep, deep wisdom of generations past, and even the energy of the cosmos can transmit through them. Reading her words, I felt an immediate resonance with these thoughts and ideas. And when I have a child one day, I intend to create a Space of Love, and also breast-feed accordingly.

Only to have a child, or even to properly nurture your inner child, you've got to sort out your relationship with yourself and others. I've

110

had many a challenge in this department; I've made many mistakes, but it's led to much learning and eventually evolutionary success. Many of the insights and techniques I've gathered in the quest to love myself and have healthy relationships are described in this next section.

PART THREE

RELATIONSHIPS

"There is no charm equal to tenderness of heart." -*Jane Austen*

To summarize it in astrological terms, I've had a cyclical journey with relationships. They started out as my Sun, making me brim with joy. Then later they acted more like my Saturn; inspiring the most challenging and painful times I've ever had. I've had to learn and grow and stretch and strengthen, and there were some good days and there were some very bad days, until eventually relationships came back to being like my Sun again. I still have my challenges of course, but lately sunny days prevail.

And it's definitely taken some big mistakes to get to this point. Sometimes I feel I've failed the tests that life has thrown at me. Yet in spite of the botches, I stop and show myself some compassion because I am human and no matter what has happened, I have evolved!

And through all the mishaps and mayhem, I managed to pick up some magical and incredible insights that I believe could help you get through your mistakes a little less tearfully and come out a little more happily.

Self-Love

Self-love is the pre-requisite for healthy relationships and pretty much anything you could ever want because when you love yourself, you take care of yourself, and you naturally do it in the best possible ways.

Only you may experience one BIG barrier to self-love, and that is self-Judgment. And in America, some of the prevalent judgments of self and others are also the most superficial ones. Our culture is unfortunately very shallow. And when most of our perceptions are based on the outside, we can easily miss the truth and the love on the inside.

In some cultures, being an elder is revered, and I long for that. I'm in my mid 30s, and it would be nice to look forward to old age as a time of my greatest honor and respect. Would that beauty be the richness of the life tapestry we weave. And instead our bodies seen as the vehicles we ride around in that will fall off in time like a shedding skin. Then perhaps one day, the world will be more conscious, and it will be more widely accepted that it is the Source within you, your Spirit, your energy, and your consciousness that is who you truly are.

So, when you look in the mirror, look past your temporary embodiment. Look through your eyes, and see your boundless spirit, your transformational soul. And when you start doing this for yourself, it will be easier to see it in others as well.

I found the Holy Grail of self-love through a channeling I attended. And the message that came through is a great one because it addresses loving yourself through the body and being the person who is beyond the body. I visited the channel after my big breakup with Steve. I was being really hard on myself and feeling very little self-love at all. It just so happened that Kuan Yin, the Goddess of Compassion, was being channeled, so I asked her, "What does it take for us to truly love ourselves?"

Practicing what she said has changed my life. The first part is to do anonymous acts of kindness. This includes things like petting a cat, sending good vibes to someone, picking up a piece of trash, etc.

Since I started consciously doing this, I realized that one of the reasons it works is that because no one else sees them, anonymous acts of kindness are in a sense gifts you give yourself. If there's no one around to praise you or give you a pat on the back or a smile for your good deed, then you will naturally give it to yourself, however subtly.

The second half of Kuan Yin's answer was this: When you finish bathing in the bath or the shower, and all makeup is washed away, go stand in the nude, look in the mirror, and practice loving yourself. This means look without judgment. However tempting, ignore the imperfections, and give yourself some praise. Just look in the mirror and love that person looking back at you.

For my part, I also believe that it helps to speak affirmations in this time. Try, "I love you. I am wonderful. I am beautiful. I am smart. I am funny." You can even post your favorite affirmations on your mirror if that helps. Tell yourself whatever it is you most want to hear; whatever you would like other people to tell you, *you* tell you. This way, you are acting as your own perfect partner before anyone else is.

Even if at first this practice is uncomfortable, keep at it because making it a habit will change your life.

Practices for Loving Yourself

- *Do anonymous acts of kindness.*
- *After bathing, while nude, send love to yourself in the mirror.*

Touching Yourself

Now let's try going further into that second aspect of self-love. In addition to expressing it verbally in the mirror, touch yourself. Try it. I mean it. *Right now.* Touch and appreciate different parts of your body. Try it with a mirror and without.

And as you touch each part of your body, speak to it. Try saying "I love you." Kiss your different parts. The cells of your body *will* respond. And it feels good! It can even feel better than kissing someone else's body because in this case, you are the direct giver and receiver of your love. Tune into that idea and emotion. It will surely help open your heart.

Loving Animals and Plants

Kuan Yin's first aspect of doing anonymous acts of kindness to further self-love can easily be explored with animals and even plants. You'll also feel the benefits immediately because pets and others will usually enjoy your attentions and then reflect them right back to you. Maybe that's one of the reasons some people are more comfortable with animals than humans. I for one totally understand loving dogs because they love so unconditionally. Both my cat and my dog have been like angels to me, and these relationships have become some of the most precious and deeply rooted bonds in my life.

I think the block that some people have with letting their love truly shine for animals is that they feel that animals aren't quite up to the standards of humans. In terms of things like overall intelligence and fine motor coordination this is often true. However, when it comes to what truly matters, this idea is selling everyone short because animals are also made of Source energy, and they are capable of deep, deep love. Therefore, they too are God-like in their own way. Loving an animal is as beautiful a communion as loving any human because love is love, and love is meant to be shared. Your love is always a gift to yourself, and it will transform you each and every time.

We are not only deeply connected and one with the animals of the Earth though, the members of the plant family are also intimately intertwined with us. They share in our oneness on this planet, and they thrive on love too. There is a reason why in experiments plants grow better when they are spoken to with love than ones who are not.

Bashar, the extra-terrestrial channeled through Darryl Anka has described our relationship with trees in a way that you may find enlightening. He says that trees act as antennae that stretch out of the Earth and pull down energy from our electromagnetic grid to bring more life to the planet.

They also form another electromagnetic grid of connecting trees from all over our planet that "supports life of all kinds." So, trees are not only giving us the breath of life, but they are also creating life energetically by bringing energy down through these antennae which provides further life support. It is no wonder that sensitive people give an inner cringe when they notice trees that are not being treated properly.

Additionally, he points out that trees are being electromagnetically and chemically bonded to us through our air exchange. Imagine molecules of air floating out of the trees and into our mouths, and vice versa. And instead of taking it for granted, acknowledge it and show gratitude. This ought to be taken into account every time people make decisions regarding the plant kingdom.

Trees and other plants are literally keeping us alive. So, to what end do we terminate their lives? Is it really worth it? Further environmental preservation would not only teach individual self-love, it would help us all on a global level.

Five Expressions of Love

Only, kind words and a soft touch are just a couple of the myriad of ways you can express your love for yourself. The others you can explore in Gary Chapman's book, "The Five Languages of Love." This book is designed to help people express and receive love to and from their partner in the most appropriate ways. These are also integral to self-love. His "Five Languages" are words of affirmation, physical touch, gifts, quality time, and acts of service.

Think about which of thee are important to you, then give these to yourself, regardless of whether you're in a partnership or not. My top two are words of affirmation and physical touch. Since realizing this about myself, I've learned to share them with me and have noticed a remarkable difference in how I feel when I do. These can be things like touching my own face. I used to long for someone to do this for me. Now I freely do it for myself, and it makes all the difference.

So, explore the Five Love Languages, and treat yourself to your favorite ways of loving. Again, look in the mirror without a stitch of clothing and connect to the infinite soul you see in your eyes. Admire the beauty in the body before you, and there is always beauty. Touch it gently and lovingly. Spend quality time with yourself and cherish it. Do something nice for you and see it as an act of love. Love yourself through your personal love languages, and also do those anonymous acts of kindness. Not only will you feel incredible, you will also able to share your beautiful energy with others just through your state of being.

Do Your Work and Others Will Follow

Yet many of us are still reluctant to love ourselves. We are uplifters. We want people to feel better, happier, more loving. Only for whatever reason, we are neglecting the cornerstone of it all: first we've got to love and uplift ourselves. And when you love yourself, you will do just that. Then naturally others will rise to a higher state when they're with you.

You see when people experience you at a high level; they have the choice to match it. Sometimes they do, and sometimes they don't. Only at least when you're up there, you have given them the opportunity, and that in and of itself is a gift.

With this in mind, as an uplifter, however busy you are, give yourself the gift of time to practice this self-care because then other people will follow. And even though it is often an unconscious choice, you will have made a difference in their lives. So, by all means, treat yourself, love yourself, and enjoy yourself. This is true power.

Now if you find yourself running into blocks, then you may be putting conditions on loving yourself. If that is the case, there is a possible solution: try remembering someone who has loved you unconditionally or whom you have loved unconditionally and take the time to feel that again.

You see once you have experienced it, the energy of unconditional love is always there in your cellular memory. All it takes is remembering, amplifying, and then turning those floodgates onto where it can be the most beneficial: you. However, it does take consistent practice. Just like with any relationship, you've got to put in the work.

I've found when it comes to unconditional love, you can be completely unconscious of your desire for it but driven to have it. I, at one time, was absolutely craving having a dog. Even though it wasn't really conducive to my lifestyle, I went out and got one from the Human Society.

I eventually realized what I had been actually longing for in a canine was unconditional love. I just wasn't getting it enough from people and I wasn't giving it to myself. Understanding that helped me to fill in the gap in other ways when the dog passed, but I had to get motivated. The insight that it was unconditional love missing made a huge difference. So, if you have blocks to loving yourself, recognize that you may have a deep emptiness within you, and have forgotten how to fill it up. Then go deep, remember, and practice. You'll get there.

It is also case in point that it's important to help our children lay the groundwork for self-love in adulthood. Teaching children to say, "I love you" and make other positive statements to themselves in the mirror, or about the Five Love Languages and how to turn them back to themselves would be an amazing next step for us all. Their practice might just start as mimicking; only eventually, as it becomes commonplace for them, they will feel comfortable doing it for themselves.

Loving Your Different Aspects

Still, you may wonder, "How do I receive love from myself?" There's just one of me, right? I can maybe understand loving my fingers and toes, but how do I as a whole person separate me out and love my whole person? Well, actually there are quite a few ways because as you will see, there are many aspects of you, and every one of them deserves love.

Let's start with the genders. You may be in a female or male body, only, the Source within you is both male and female. So, when you're contemplating varying ways of loving yourself, why not try it from either the male or female counterpart within you? For instance, when you're doing the mirror exercise, caressing yourself, or talking to yourself, experiment with doing it from and to either or both genders, i.e. female to female, female to male part, male to male, or male to female, and feel the varying types of feeling. This isn't an exercise in sexuality per say, although it can be. It is about connecting with, understanding, and loving the different parts of you according to gender.

You can also do this from the vantage point of your different personalities. Many people aren't aware that we are made up of different personalities. This isn't an obvious feature in a human because when they are all integrated within you, they manifest seamlessly, and usually only shines forth at a time. When it actually is apparent that a person has multiple personalities is when they are segregated, as in mental illness, and you hardly recognize one personality from another.

So, once you've digested the idea that we all have different personalities, but more than likely have them all sewn together, try loving yourself to and from these different parts: the funny you loving the serious you, the joyful you loving the quizzical you. Love yourself collapsed in a heap crying on your bed. Love yourself relaxing after a long day's work. Love yourself struggling to control your temper. Love yourself feeling elated at the sight of someone you love. See, recognize and hold each of your natures in your consciousness. Be with them as you live by stepping outside of yourself and bearing witness to what's going on within you. The love can and will flow as you appreciate your distinctive makeups.

And yet a further way to love your different aspects is to love yourself throughout time. Since all time is one*, and we exist in different timeframes, a person can love their child self as their older self, or love their older self as their younger self, their selves in other dimensions, their future-life selves, their past-lives selves...The list goes on and on. And these selves may already love one another consciously or otherwise.

There can be Love connections all throughout a person. Nevertheless, as you very well know, we are not usually conscious of ourselves as different selves because that is not generally how the game of Earth is played. However, awareness that we are different people, and setting the intention of seeing with eyes of love towards any other self that you are can help you expand and heal.

I recently did an exercise where I stepped outside of myself and looked back at me. Then I asked "How would I feel about this person if she were not me? "   This was interesting to imagine and contemplate because a different type of compassion and love emerged than I had ever felt for myself before. It seems that I am not as quick to judge when I step out and look in. When I look at myself with my tragedies and triumphs, I feel a different type of compassion than me looking in at me.

Try this in contemplation, and you may notice some of your usual judgments giving way to further acceptance because we often don't hold others to the same standard we hold ourselves to.

"When a stream comes to some stones in its path, it doesn't struggle to remove them, or fight against them, or think about them. It just goes around them. And as it does, it sings. -"The Tao of Piglet"

*See the Time in Now and DNA Chapter

Different Ways to Love Your Many Selves

- *From Gender to Gender*
- *From Personality to Personality*
- *To and From Different Ages, Times, and Dimensions*
- *To and From Inside and Outside of Yourself*

Loving and Accepting the Shadow Self

One thing you may have noticed in life and as you contemplate the different aspects of yourself that need love is that there are certain temperaments within you that you really aren't as fond of as others. Any personality you're not comfortable with is usually an aspect of your Shadow Self. The Shadow Self is made up of the parts of you that you're embarrassed by, that you might even hate, that you wish you could sweep under a rug and never see...Nevertheless; no part of you should be discounted. In fact, it is harmful to do so. Again, every aspect deserves to be loved.

This is where it gets tough though. It is difficult to go where the shame and the guilt hide. People rarely want to team up with those characters, let alone send them love. Instead they prefer to bury them behind smiles or a stonewall. Unfortunately, when you try to keep the Shadow Self hidden out of fear of hurting or being hurt you can also end up abandoning it. And this is the last piece of you that you want to dismiss. It can and will come up with a vengeance.

Let me give you an example. When my partner's adult daughter, Natalie, lived with us, I thought I would be the perfect mother for her. I was in love with her dad, and I thought I would love her just as deeply. We would be a family. Then, as anyone could have expected, she and I got into a big fight. I was really hurt, and I'm sure she was too. Only instead of working it out with her, I told her to give me some space. I mistakenly believed that if I just didn't interact with her, there would be no more conflict. Only there was. I hadn't forgiven her for what she said, and she was still holding some grievances about me. So, our buried feelings ended up reemerging later like the gopher in the children's game that keeps popping up unexpectedly. The players have to keep bopping it down, only to find it pops up again. This is what happened to us with our shadows. And it was miserable for me.

The whole time she lived with us I was in therapy trying to learn tolerance for her when it would have been more beneficial to have been exploring and loving my own shadows. I did get a lot better acquainted with my Shadow Self because she did not stay where I put her during the six months Natalie stayed with us, and I was embarrassed by my behavior for just as long afterwards.

So, if you find yourself hiding the negative parts of your personality, pick them back up. They are lonely, and to abandon these babies will lead to less authenticity and lowered self-esteem.

Not loving it is like not loving a part of our body. When you disavow love to one part of your body it affects your attitude towards your whole body. Further, attempting to cut off your Shadow Self is as disastrous as cutting off a piece of your body you don't like. True, the part you didn't like would be gone, only you would be maimed. So, the next time, your Shadow Self steps forward, bares its teeth and roars its ugly head, take a deep breath. 'Oh my God. Here I am again.' Acknowledge that attitude, or lack-there-of, similar to how you would a temperamental baby...Show some compassion. Love it! Laugh at it and speak to it playfully. It might look back at you baffled, but then it will gently crawl back towards you, and wait to be invited into your lap. Then, together you can reintegrate back into the fold of who you are and shine brighter than ever.

Caroline Myss explains integrating the Shadow Self well in her book, *Defy Gravity*.

"No one lives just in the light, any more than he lives just in the dark...The day contains the night and the night always moves into the day, like the black dot within the white swirl of the yin-yang symbol. The same is true of our natures."

In this world of duality, wouldn't it make sense for us who contain both light and dark to accept it just like we do with any other animal? Shine the Light of acknowledgement and acceptance on it and feel the love that your darkness has been missing.

Fear of Loving Thy Self

The fear of the Shadow Self may not be the only thing that affects your willingness to love yourself, however. You also may fear losing others' approval if you step out of the ordinary, if you change. Only it can't be helped. Change is inevitable, and although most flow in and out with the tides of others, and even if given the choice wouldn't prefer individual evolution if it meant risking relationships, sometimes you just get swept up and end up far out to sea. Only once you when learn to swim in the deep, you will never be content with just the shoreline again.

Transformational love, though it is risky and takes courage, can be the most extraordinary and beautiful experience. Only people can be resistant, and you may be one. You could be afraid to love yourself and truly be yourself because you've been brought up with other people who do not love themselves and loving themselves. Maybe they carry deep shame. Maybe it's carried through generations. And just maybe these are the ones you love the best, your own friends and family. Naturally you fear that when you love yourself that you're going to be met with some resistance. So, it's scary, and initially is not the easiest course of action. Only it *does* turn out to be the best.

Have the awareness that there will always be people with many different opinions and they're not all going to align with what you do and who you are when you love yourself and are being our truest self. Only you can't let that hamper your flow. Instead choose compassion and forgiveness through the understanding that the resentment they feel is from the unconscious realization that you are doing something that they too long deeply to do. And yet, they are denying themselves. It is really frustrating. However when you keep living in that space of self-love you give them the opportunity to feel it secondhand, which also gives them the chance to snap out of the lull they're in. And this is a chance they might not otherwise have had.

Acceptance and Responsibility

Getting to a place of self-love can be tough. Life has thrown some challenges at me, and sometimes I feel like I've made a mess of them. I understand how it feels to be healing a wound and go to that place of hurt, dwelling in the anger, pain and shame that still reside there. It is the rational thing to do when I notice a wound that is continuing to negatively affect my life. Only I've also found instead of dwelling, I can lift up the stains, heal the pain, and integrate the experiences into the beautiful thread of my life. And one of the first steps here is to accept what happened.

This can be difficult. In the face of pain, your instinct may be to behave like a wounded dog, snarling and biting, retreating farther back into yourself. And yet these defense mechanisms can be diffused by acceptance, which is really just standing back from the experience, looking at it as an observer, and thinking, 'Yes, this happened.'

The next step in healing emotional wounds is claiming responsibility. This can be equally challenging. It is so easy to play the blame game, but blaming others is not going to prevent an event from happening again. Taking responsibility for the part you played in it will. Remember it takes two to tango. Ask yourself, "How did I find myself here?" and "What would I do differently next time?" When you zoom out and look at it from a higher perspective, you will see how the experience could have originated from within yourself.

For my part, I kept having different women in my family insult me in a similar way, and I felt like I'd done little to nothing wrong except express myself. My therapist finally asked me, "Why are you having them hold up this mirror to you?" What was obvious to her was that I was provoking them to this end because there was something I wanted to see about myself, a shadow that I was unwilling to recognize otherwise. It was through this lens that I took responsibility when I would usually otherwise claim victimhood.

Yet another perspective on why people have bad experiences comes from Abraham, the wise group of benevolent beings channeled by Esther Hicks. Abraham talks about how even at a young age, we attract some really awful experiences. You know, the "Why did this happen to me?" ones. Many of us have had them and really just want them to heal.

Only they are so awful and unexpected that we can hold onto the fear for the rest of our lives if we allow ourselves to. Abraham-Hicks's perspective is to realize that those experiences are actually teachers in that they provide a stark contrast to what we do want. And having a greater awareness of what we would love helps creates it. For instance, children who watched their parents go through a messy divorce can see clearly that they want peace and equanimity even in parting.

I've taken this idea into my own life, and I no longer feel like a victim of circumstance. Regarding my own "dark night of the soul," I too used to ask myself "Why did this happen to me?" It seems like that much suffering wasn't justified. Only it helps to remember all the things that I learned during that period. And perhaps my soul needed it. Maybe it grew from it. And maybe because of that, all that drama was actually a beautiful and interesting part of my life.

It's like being a preteen or a teenager and first experiencing anxiety and self-loathing. The contrast of the darkness makes the light and carefree times of childhood and being a teenager appear to shine so much brighter.

So when you look back at those things that have brought you suffering instead of pleasure, try to see how much you have grown from them on a personal level, and then recognize that even though you may not be consciously aware of your soul's growth, it is there and it is important.

This is part of the paradox of living here in this world of duality, what some might believe is the worst part of their lives, on another level, is their best because that's when they grew the most. I'm not saying here to go out and create suffering for the purpose of growth. I'm just pointing out that you can be okay with what has already happened because there is always some gift that flows from these things; always some lesson to learn.

Step 1: Accept whatever happened; good or bad and see how this circumstance contributed to your soul's growth.

Step 2: Look back at the time surrounding the circumstances, and ask yourself, "How did I feel? "

Step 2 is important because the people we have had a conflict with could never have had that interaction with us if we had not on some level given them permission. And part of the way we do so is through the vibration we emitted around that time, which stemmed from our thoughts and emotions.

Acknowledging that your vibration could be a contributing factor, and recognizing it for what it was will help you to try to remember to monitor your vibration more closely next time.)

Some refer to the attraction of negativity due to our energy field as karma. (Here we are addressing events that occur due to karma in this lifetime because it is more recognizable. This differs from the karma that seems to occur out of the blue because it was created on another timeline and is not readily accessible by our conscious minds.)

Therefore, it's important to recognize that if we'd kept our vibration higher, we wouldn't have even been in that space. The others involved might have bounced right off of our energy fields like bubbles, gone around, or in some cases not even have seen us.

So to move forward, first acceptance is often key. It helps to neutralize what happened and then we can begin to move forward and do marvelous things. Sometimes that's all that it takes, being okay with what happened and then taking a bit of responsibility that allows us to swing past the drama and be the true creators that we are.

The young entrepreneur who started GoPro, Nick Woodman, wasn't wrapped up in his hurts when he started his business, and he had already had one business fail. Instead he put it behind him, went on a surfing adventure, and it was there that he got the GoPro idea.

And that's where we have to also be in order to let go and live on the edge of the next wave. Acceptance and responsibility will help us to get there.

Making the Match

Once you're fully on the path to self-acceptance and self-love, it may be time to find a partner to share your life with. I've been one of those people who has gone from person to person; not finding a keeper for the longest, and it has been frustrating. I, finally, at this moment, am with my first partner, Napoleon, who has lasted longer than a year. We're going on four now, and it is amazing to continue sharing this joy and intimacy. It is just getting deeper and deeper. Every day he blesses me with his love, I bless him with mine, we bless our dog and cat with both of ours, and we are grateful.

But before him, I went round and round through several men. Each time I was hoping I'd found the right one, and each time I got disappointed. Nevertheless, each of these individuals had different things to teach me, and different characteristics that I liked. The trouble was finding them all in one man. I was also getting tired of all the drama that comes with going from relationship to relationship. Thankfully, I learned to focus better. This helped me to narrow in on Napoleon, and although he comes with his own set of challenges, it is all worth it to share my life with him.

So, the reason that focusing on the positive aspects of every partner works is because when you focus on what you love about another, those aspects are also activated in you. And what's activated in you will magnetize people of similar characteristics. Try it and recognize each person as your partner in self-discovery and growth, until one day, you find someone who checks all the right boxes. He or she will indeed be everything you've wanted and probably more. Through the Relationship Focus Technique the dating game is almost like a buffet. It gives you room to appreciate what you've had and also to try new things. For example, you know you like chocolate, so why not try the chocolate mousse? It could become your favorite dessert.

Also sometimes you don't always know what you want until you've had what you don't want. So, date and find out. Enjoy the experience. This is why people love online dating so much. It gives them the opportunity to see what's out there and narrow it down because they have experienced such a wide assortment of people. So, allow your journey of dating to also be a path of self-discovery.

The Relationship Focus Technique will help you to adore the process of refining and finding love for you.

The Relationship-Focus Technique

With potential partners you date, focus on what you love about them. This is not to discount what you don't like about them. You just don't put a lot of energy into those aspects. Even after you've let them go, continue to focus on their positive points whenever you think of them.

Note additional characteristics you haven't even experienced yet to add to your list. Continue to refine yourself so that you can more easily be a match to this ideal. Then you'll more easily attract someone who is the compilation of all the traits you've been contemplating.

"The One"

Only when you are with a wonderful match that you feel like you could spend the rest of your life with, please be flexible. In other words, there may be more to this equation than you've been led to believe, so don't put too much stock in finding the infamous "One" or being with the "One" for your whole life.

I, like most Millennials, was brought up on a series of Disney princesses, and somewhere along the line, I started believing that all I had to do to live happily ever after was find my Prince. Several years ago, I was sure I'd found him. Steve was sensitive, kind, loving; a beautiful person, and I thought I loved him more than anyone else in the world.

Only things changed between us. First I quit my job and was having a difficult time getting over it. That combined with my dad's passing the year before was affecting my mental health. It was around this time that he decided he no longer wanted to be with me. My "One" no longer desired me.

I kept myself miserable for an entire year hoping he would come back to me. In the meantime, I was doing everything I could to change myself, make myself better; to make myself into the kind of person person that this wouldn't happen to.

I waited and waited. I called him every now and then and left messages. On Christmas Eve, I even left a bundle of presents on his doorstep; spending my last dollars on him so that somehow someway he might have me again. A week later he left me a voicemail saying he didn't love me anymore. I was already starting to shift, and that brought me a little more closure, and yet still I hung on. He was my "One" and I stubbornly wouldn't rest until we were together again.

This is what mistaken beliefs can do to you. They can turn you into a crazy person with no self-esteem and no self-worth.

My therapist, God bless her, convinced me to put a cap on all that waiting. I decided on my birthday. I didn't hear from him, and it turned out to be a wonderful birthday. I was letting go. I was finally free, and transforming into the new, independent woman I had been envisioning myself as. It was then, as I stepped out of my yearlong cocoon that I realized all the changes I'd thought I'd been making for him, were actually changes for me. And, ironically enough, it turned out they were also helping me to move past him.

To fully get over it though, I had to form some new belief systems. First, I decided that life didn't have to revolve around being in the right relationship and making a family. It did not have to be my be-all and my end-all. Instead I decided my life would be about serving the world and helping out wherever I feel inspired.

The other realization I had was that him not wanting me didn't actually have a whole lot to do with me at all. His choices were about what he wanted for his own life, which I found out later did not include a family. So, if he didn't want a family, or me then he was actually not the "One" for me at all, and it was up to me to figure out what I wanted from my life, independent of his. These are feminist tenants that I'd heard of, but I guess I had to learn them from the School of Hard Knocks to really understand them.

Looking back, it is all common sense, but hindsight is 20/20, and I loved that man. When they say love is blind, I can now affirm that that is very, very true.

Nonetheless, since then, I get over the ending of relationships a lot more quickly, partially because I don't want to waste all that time and energy pining away. I simply have better things to do. If it's not right, I accept it and move on no matter how much I love him.

Looking back, from one perspective, the whole experience seems like a heck of a waste of a year. From another, however, I became a whole lot stronger. Now, I feel I can honestly say, I spent a year going back and forth to hell, and now I'm ready to stay on Earth and make it Heaven.

The moral of the story is that there are actually many, many, potential partners for us. Please don't buy into those Disney stories. I know they're fed to us from a young age but try to resist! Cinderella, Snow White, Sleeping Beauty; they all actually had thousands of true love princes available to them. Disney didn't show it, but if need be, there was always another one right around the corner. In other words, you can have that love again, but don't be uptight about the face that it comes with.

Additionally, let's continue to relax the whole man-wife, together-forever paradigm we've been raised with. Relationship types are as varied as individuals. We all do it differently, for different lengths of time, and with different results. Every relationship is a success, however painful, because we learn from them. The life lessons are the reward.

It's also helpful to understand that people change. The person that you are now is not who you'll be tomorrow, next month, and especially not years from now. Therefore, the idea that getting married is the only key to living happily ever after is bullocks. Why hold your future self to a vow when your future wants, and desires may be totally different from what they are now? You may grow together, and you may grow apart. Under those future circumstances, doesn't marriage seem like a pretty risky gamble?

So, give yourselves the freedom to evolve in whatever way is best for you. Marriage can be like a security blanket for some people, and after 4 years with talk of having kids, I'm leaning towards it myself, but Love doesn't need the bonds of marriage to be all that we ever wanted. Modern times and new ways of living are giving us more freedom than that.

Gracefully Separating

So how long do you allow yourself to live unhappily before you separate from a partner that is no longer good for you? I waited unhappily a year after Steve, and I had broken up. Talk about a misplaced loyalty.

The channel, Abraham-Hicks advises giving it a week, and leaving when you are in sync with yourself, so that you are running *to* something, not away from something. And I have to say that I heartily agree. I've told my partner this too. Coincidentally, his moods never last longer than 5 days. Granted, practicing this is easier when you are not married, and do not have kids. Only, think of the freedom that comes from just giving it a week. No longer do you have to wait around, hang around when you already know that you're unhappy. You can say, "Sure, we've been together for a while, but I need more love. So rather than spinning this round and round another 7X7 times, I'm going to move on." Then you can cut the cords and move onto your next great adventure with your next great partner.

Breaking up may be easier if you remind yourself that you can only change yourself, so it's okay to let go. You resonate with thousands of people on a romantic level, so put a limit on the amount of time that you'll allow yourself to suffer. Give yourself the chance to be happier. The Earth doesn't need any more martyrs. It needs more heroes.

Releasing the Relationship Ceremony

Now if you are in the stage of being out of a relationship, and yet still holding on, this next practice will get you through it. I know because when I was still holding onto my relationship with Steve, this ceremony is what finally got me over it.

It can also take doing this ceremony more than once if you are stubbornly holding onto someone. It may help to remind yourself that when you do finally let them go; you'll have a cleaner energy field, so expect a much better match when you're ready.

Releasing the Relationship Ceremony

Write out the story of your relationship; the emotions you felt then and now, and how you intend to let go of the present relationship through the ceremony.

Preferably go out into nature. Open your ceremony by bowing to the directions, and then bringing the energy into your heart.

State your intention and burn the story you wrote out.

As you are burning the papers, fan the smoke out, up, and away from you. (This is releasing that energy you were holding in your field out into the ethers.)

Refill your energy field with energy from Source by turning on your Light, or absorb energy from nature.

Close the ceremony the way you began it.

The refilling your energy part is very important because following the burning there will be a void there in your energy field. Unless you fill the void first with Love, Source energy, Nature or what-have-you, the universe will fill it for you. So not filling it is kind of hit-or-miss.

Also, be aware that when you release a lot of emotional stuff, there will likely be some major shifting in your energy field. Expect to go through some pretty intense emotions. In the time to come, you may choose to warn the people you'll be around or decide to take some time for yourself during processing.

Reclaiming your Pieces

And yet another great tool to help you move on from past relationships and step into an even fuller version of who you are is reclaiming the pieces of yourself that you left in these different relationships.

This answer that you might not have even known you were asking is from a question a friend of mine had at the channeling I used to attend. She said she felt like a chameleon, like she was just blending in with whomever she was with. She didn't really feel like she knew who she was anymore, and couldn't understand how it had happened. The reason she was given through the channel was that she had left a piece of herself behind in nearly every person with whom she'd had a close, intimate relationship.

My friend was told that once she called these pieces back to herself, she would have more of herself and would feel whole again.

When I heard this, I was entranced, and also a little irritated because I had a hunch that there were people with whom I was no longer in contact walking around with pieces of me that would be better suited for me. So, I immediately went to work on it that night.

And every morning following this practice, I felt more like myself. I have done this exercise many times. Following every breakup, and nearly every ended friendship, I reclaim me for me. And now, I am able to stand strongly in who I am.

Reclaiming Your Pieces

Before you go to sleep, pick one person you've had a relationship with. Perhaps you feel things are still unfinished with them. Perhaps you miss them, and yet being together is no longer an option. Ask to have the pieces of you that you left behind with them to come back.

Ask for only one person at a time.

Don't feel guilty about taking back parts of you. You're not taking back all the love you shared with them, just the parts that rightfully belong to you.

Healing and Reinventing Yourself

And once you do let go of a relationship that is no longer serving you why not use that time and space to reinvent yourself? You'll have more fun, and attract an entirely different partner the next time around.

Reinventing yourself is brilliant, and fun to do. When you're no longer in a relationship, it leaves a big space in your life. That's when it's a good time to ask yourself, "What kind of person do I want to fill this void?"

I once met a guy who after his divorce made a list of everything he wanted in a woman, and then a second list of everything he needed to be in order to attract this woman of his dreams. Within a year, he visited an organic farm on Maui, and sure enough, fell for his tour guide. Soon after, they moved back together to his farm in Connecticut as cute and happy as they could be.

My grandfather did not do that. After my grandmother died of cancer he was devastated, so he did what many older men do, he immediately moved onto the next woman he could find. She ended up spending all his money and leaving him penniless.

So, before you move along to the next one, and I know rebounding can be fun, just make sure that you've learned what you needed to learn, and healed, so you can usher in a whole new chapter in your life.

And one excellent way to reinvent yourself is through travel. Travel is an excellent investment in yourself because being out of your element helps you to live in the present, an especially good place to be when you're dealing with a breakup, and you can't help but be changed by it.

According to Bashar, the extra-terrestrial channeled by Darryl Anka, there is actually a formula that defines everything and one of the variables to that formula is location. Therefore, if you change a person's location variable, then you also change the person. In other words, you are a completely different individual depending entirely on where you are.

Although in the future people will understand this like second nature, it's important for us to recognize it now so that we feel freer to give ourselves this additional evolutionary tool. So, if changing locations can help you transform when you're getting over a breakup, albeit temporarily, I would say go for it. There may even be a location that would most assist you in becoming your ideal self, and that's up for exploration.

Getting back to basics in healing after a relationship, I feel that exercise is key. I'll run nearly every day. The cardio jump-starts my heart again, and keeps it beating, literally and figuratively. The exercise also helps clear the chakras.

Reading transports. This can be so helpful in the transition period, especially if you have a busy mind. I recommend sweet, juicy fiction that keeps your mind out of the worrying and obsessing phases, or self-help if you're feeling reflective. Just keep your mind occupied so that it stays away from worry and regret. Don't be afraid to read whatever strikes your fancy until your vibration is consistently high again.

Moreover, if you find yourself still holding onto your ex like some sort of worn out blanket, there is also a beautiful, powerful affirmation you can do to help you to move on. Say to this person, out loud or in your mind, "I bless you, and I release you." I had to say this to the second person and only American that I'd slept with hundreds of times across space and time in order to finally let him go. I was *very* attached. Through this affirmation, I went from being mildly depressed to not even thinking about him in a short period of time.

Forgiveness

"I am no longer willing to carry around pain in response to your actions."

-Doreen Virtue

Forgiveness is key to healing and reinventing yourself. It is also one of the hardest. Our egos can easily create a resistance to it because we are afraid of getting hurt again. It's a messed up form of self-preservation: never get hurt again, but never truly love again either. Instead of preventing suffering, the grudges actually draw it out. The hurt might not be as intense as it was initially; only the dull ache of resentment remains.

I know that ache very well, and compounded it is not fun. Some years back I was taking issue with a lot of people at once, including family members; going around with so much bitterness in my heart, it was nearly insufferable. So, I prayed, and I prayed, and I believe that when a person really needs something, and asks for it, the universe provides. It did.

But first, I needed to have a realization. You see while I was focusing on the wrongs that people had done to me; swimming uncomfortably in a sea of victimhood, I lost something that I had previously taken for granted: my sense of peace and happiness. When I realized that these were missing, and had been for a while, I was even more motivated to do something about my lack of forgiveness.

So, if you too are feeling resentful, remember a couple of things: first, your natural inclination is to fall towards love. And second, when you are in a loving state, you are being your true self. Therefore, when you begrudge someone, you are not allowing yourself to be who you truly are. You are holding you apart from you all in the name of protection.

It's not like we have a whole herd of role models showing us how to do this either. One of the problems with our society is we're so used to not falling towards love that it's considered normal, and people sometimes mistake things that are normal for being good. That is obviously not always true.

If you want to forgive, yet still feel scared of repeated injury, then you take heart by taking space, and being at peace from afar. Let me give you an example. There was a time when my mom and I were not getting along at all. Every time we saw each other, it was the same old painful pattern. Finally, I decided, 'She is really the only person I am having these problems with, so it must be our chemistry. I've had enough. I'm going to leave her in peace and live in my own peace.' And so I did. I took about 6 months off from seeing her. And in that time, I worked on myself, reflected, and shifted into a lighter person.

By the time we saw each other again, the destructive pattern from before was broken. We had learned to accept one another and not take each other so seriously. And in the light-heartedness, came forgiveness. We were harmonious once again.

She told me later that she had asked herself, 'Why is my daughter keeping away from me?' She spoke to her therapist about it, and then reevaluated some of her own actions.

And I was doing my own work. In that interlude, I had done a visualization to help me to forgive my mom, and quite a few other people for that matter. It is done with the assistance of angels. If you are a person who doesn't quite believe in angels, then ask to be given proof of their existence, and proof will come. Just try not to discount it when it does.

Angelic Forgiveness Visualization

The Angelic Forgiveness Visualization works through the manipulation of energy chords. These form when people exchange energy. You can learn more about them in Barbara Brennan's book, *Hands of Light*.

When you are in a state of discord with someone it is because some of these chords between you could use some refining. Cleaning them up and eliminating others can help pave the way for a whole new relationship. The beautiful thing about energy, and more specifically, energetic chords, is that with practice, you can actually feel them.

The visualization at the end of this section is super effective because you are not only forgiving the person with whom you're in a relationship, you are also facilitating forgiveness *from* them.

There are two different statements that you can use in this visualization.

This first one comes from the Pranic Healing Teacher, Master Stephen Co. It is also a wonderful statement to us because instead of remaining whole-heartedly in a space of blame, it adds compassion and unity to your quiver.

"Namaste. Salutation to the Divinity in you. We are all children of God. We all make mistakes. We are all evolving... You are forgiven. I ask for your forgiveness too. Blessings be upon you. Go in peace."

The second is a reminder that you had expectations, and this person did not meet them. Therefore, begrudging them is unnecessary.

"I forgive you for not being the person I wanted you to be. I forgive you and I set you free."

Before or even during this exercise you may feel some reluctance. Letting go of expectations can be difficult. My mom was one of the hardest people I've ever forgiven. Part of me did not want to let those grievances go. Though I knew full well she was a good person, what had happened between us, especially since my dad had passed, was painful! Thoughts flew through my mind like, 'Will she do it again if I let my guard down?' and 'I don't want to have to hurt like that anymore.'

Only I recognized and continue to recognize how important forgiveness is not only for the clearance of my heart, but also for my whole being. I persevered on. I kept at forgiving. It's just what you gotta do, and as you go on forgiving, you'll find yourself getting stronger, more flexible. And it gets easier. It's like working out. Let that be your incentive as you forgive.

Sometimes the person you haven't forgiven is someone you may quite frankly never care to see again. If this is the case, remember that through forgiving them, you can release them with a lasting sense of peace that will benefit you both in the long run.

Also, even if you don't get it all done in one round, please try again. You'll know if the resentment is still there by that painful itch. As you persevere though, you'll see the grudges melting away and they'll be replaced with peace, compassion and understanding.

Angelic Forgiveness Visualization

Call the energy of the person you are forgiving to you by speaking or thinking their name 3 times.

Imagine an angel behind you, and an angel behind them.

See each angel working with the energetic chords between you. See them burning, smoothing, and cutting them. As you watch them work on the cords, think or say to the person,

"Namaste. Salutation to the Divinity in you. We are all children of God. We all make mistakes. We are all evolving... You are forgiven. I ask for your forgiveness too. Blessings be upon you. Go in peace."

And/Or

"I forgive you for not being the person I wanted you to be. I forgive you and I set you free."

Building the Road to Contact:
Shifting a Painful Experience

This next exercise is a supplement for the forgiveness visualization. When you have had a traumatic experience with someone, and then associate the trauma with him or her, it can then be difficult to interact lovingly. Only you may still want them around because there is genuine love between you.

I've had to do this with my partner's mother. It's been tough because when I remembered the incident that hurt me, my heart would tighten. immediately and I wasn't a comfortable with that. But I stuck with this visualization time and again, and afterwards I felt a little more relaxed and gentler with her. It's taken time and effort, but the path to genuine forgiveness has being laid. The following visualization will make it easier for you too to share space again by energetically allaying the original trauma.

Shifting a Painful Experience

Take some deep breaths and go back in your mind to when the trauma occurred.

Spin some loving pink energy around the time frame. It is almost like you're inside the frame of a picture or inside a snow globe. (The loving pink energy may look like cotton candy.) Watch it seep into and fill the space.

Repeat this every day until you feel intuitively that things have shifted to support interacting again in a healthy, loving manner.

Helping Another Shift their Energy for Contact

The following visualization is also great for opening the door to people whom you have hurt or have been hurt by. While previously you shifted the energy of a past event to make contact easier, this one assists the energy of the person whom you would like to be more receptive.

It is simple and only takes a minute. You'll feel a shift when you're with them partially because wounds are healing more fluidly. Additionally, if letting you go out of their life is something that they've been considering, they may be less likely to choose that.

Side note: The above exercises are designed to make it easier for you to forgive people, particularly while those said are still alive. It is more effective to do so while you are all still in body because it helps everyone to heal and evolve while you're on Earth. And although it is much more difficult than when they're in spirit because we tend to take things extremely personally here, it is well worth it.

Nevertheless, if there is someone who has already passed over whom you need to forgive, the angelic forgiveness visualization will still work its magic, as will Shifting a Negative Experience and Helping Another Shift their Energy for Contact.

Helping Another Shift their Energy for Contact

Every day for a week before meeting or calling them, see a bail of universal love around the person.

Rewriting History

If this is new for you, you may find you've let things go for so long that you don't even remember whom you need to forgive and why. This is understandable. When you get caught up in the business of life buried resentments can be easy to ignore. This won't last forever however. Little things will come up to trigger you, reminding you that you have work to do work on and that it's about time to heal.

If what you're healing is buried so deeply that you don't remember, consider asking your Higher Self and Spirit Guides* to provide you with the information you need in your meditation and dreams to heal.

In going the dream route, remember that dreams can be ridiculously tricky because some will be part of your subconscious acting itself out; sometimes reflecting the fear and worry of the day, some will be hints of what you've been up to in your sleep state, and then, some could be clues from your guides.

Regardless, write your dreams down immediately upon waking. Even if you only remember a snippet, write it out because the act of writing will connect you more and more to your waking subconscious. My dream journal resembles a crow's beak scrawling across the pages, but because I want to remember that altered state, I keep at it.

You'll be surprised by some of the hidden messages, but don't take every little thing seriously. As a rule, ignore nightmares. On the other hand, if a dream is just a little raw, and you feel it gets at the heart of you, you may want to reflect on it.

When you identify your issues, where they came from, and heal them, you will find that you don't cycle through the same drama over and over again You will have sealed the cracked foundation. And when there's another opportunity, will take a better suited path for you. Ultimately, your present will be happier and more peaceful.

I explored this dream technique one night before sleep when I wasn't acting in harmony with my boyfriend. And what did my dreams reveal? But a painful encounter I'd had with my aunt and uncle. Somehow, I realized I was associating the two.

The technique I used to heal the incident with my relatives so I could then have a better time with my boyfriend is called Rewriting History. This is not to imply that you forget what happened. No, it's quite the contrary. You rewrite it and remember it both ways.

Rewriting history may appear to be a silly concept, even though it's already been done quite a lot. However, how we remember the past changes our present, and therefore retelling a memory in a nicer, kinder way, can benefit you immensely.

Remembering the past in more than one way, and letting the compassionate one, who we *wished* we'd been, what we *wish* we'd done be the one that's superimposed over the other will help us to move past the old paradigm. Hence, painting a nicer, kinder picture of experiences helps us to step into the nicer, kinder version of ourselves.

Allow me to go a bit further in this explanation in terms of the circle of time we already discussed. If the past is actually mutable, and time runs in a circle**, then you can change it by thinking about the past as you would the future, as you would have liked for it to happen. This changes your present, which then shifts your future and then your past.

This concept illustrates differently as a spiral. A spiral goes in a circle, and each time the line comes around to a certain point, you are faced with a choice. It may not be exactly same choice, but it will be a very similar one. If you have already rewritten the past, then your new choices are going to be foremost on your mind, not your past "failures." Chances are you'll make the new and better choice at the next spiral turn.

Remember, after all, a mistake is really a mis-take. If the film isn't quite right, you just do another take. It can be the same with our lives. There is no use in beating yourself up for a mistake. It is healthier that you just see what you want to change and "Take Two."

I recently rewrote history when I was haunted by my choices and their seemingly insufficient consequences. I was on vacation on a secluded farm housesitting, and in that quiet, the memories were all coming to me at once. I felt so depressed, which is not how I had expected to feel on vacation. However, I also felt like I was being reminded that I needed healing on these issues, and I had a great opportunity to address them in such a healing setting.

So, I had a conversation with myself. 'What can I do about this? I'm still suffering over these things, and I'm feeling wretched. I must still have something to learn from them. It would benefit me to grow from them. What's the best way to do so? Moving forward, since I wish I had done it differently, how would I change things if I had a crack at them again?

And then, in an effort to move past the past, and grow into the full, confident woman that I am, I sat down and I rewrote history.

It changed me. I felt lighter, and I stopped going over the same regrets and mistakes. I feel more confident. When I freed my mind, I freed myself.

*See the Spirit Guides Chapter

**See the Time Is Now and DNA Chapter

Rewrites

Rewrite how you would like to do over your mistakes.

Write the new experiences as if they actually happened that way.

Burn your rewrites in ceremony; lifting the smoke up to the ethers where you want to make your imprint.

Also try this one:

The Law of Three

Go back in your mind to a recent mistake.

See yourself doing it the way you would have preferred to do it 3 times.

Feel the peace that results.

Rewrites and The Law of Three are two great practices because they will not only put your mind at ease about the past, but they will also solidify what you are learning.

Calming Anger

Nevertheless, a lot of these regrettable experiences could be avoided if we just learned to control our anger. Growing up, people in my family would love to say that they had a hot temper, which then gave them space to abdicate responsibility. "Oh, she just has an Irish temper," my relatives would say about whoever was blowing their fuse at the time. "We all do." As if it was perfectly healthy and normal. What they were not taking into account, but I would eventually realize, is that acting out in anger, regardless of genetics, is still a choice.

I'm not discounting anger as an important and telling emotion. When a person gets angry, that initial spark is a message from their Higher Self. However, the moments of anger last about 15 seconds; long enough to breathe through it. After that, if you choose to continue to feel that way, it's you who is fanning the flames through negative judgment. In other words, a temper may be quick to boil, but it need not boil for long.

In those early 15 seconds, you actually have the choice of whether or not to act on the anger. And the time to make that choice is usually in the split second right after the anger has arisen: the exact time when you want to act on it.

You may notice that people who are prone to act on anger do so because they enjoy the release and the powerful feeling. When in fact, acting on anger can actually be disempowering. When a person goes all out on their emotions instead of allowing their mental faculties to temper the passion; their frontal brain becomes flooded with blood. This in turn decreases the blood flow to the other parts of the brain that are in charge of rational thinking. Then they'll say and do a whole lot of things that they wouldn't have done had they thought it through. This is ultra-destructive to relationships not to mention to one's health.

Nonetheless, this behavior is also super-preventable. So how do you prevent acting in anger?

In the split second of anger where you get to decide whether to blow up or not, take 10 deep breaths. Those breaths will supply oxygen to your brain, and you will start to think more clearly. The breaths will also decrease the amount of the stress hormone, cortisol. Cortisol is a hormone that contributes to Alzheimer's, so the less you allow it to seep into your brain, the better. If all of us who have ever acted in anger, instead chose to take 10 deep breaths before acting, the world would indeed be a better place.

Calming Anger

In the split second after becoming angry, take 10 deep breaths, and then act.

When you do this, you'll find your relationships will deepen and your decision-making skills will improve.

Having Compassion and Forgiving Yourself

It is important to remember when you are out there in the world that you may have been given some inaccurate roadmaps. Some are falsified, half-done, even guessed, and there are some that you can't actually see. So, if you get lost and make mistakes, know that it wasn't really your fault. And although you may intuitively realize this already, it's still easy and counterproductive to be hard on yourself.

So rather than berating yourself which can hurt you even more, slow down your healing process, and keep you from moving forward, appreciate the experience for what it was: a lesson. And move on! Then it will become easier to show yourself some compassion as you might easily do for someone else who did something similar and had it backfire, the poor soul. When you allow them in your shoes, you may find it easier to allow the compassion to flow through you and back again like a spiritual boomerang.

If I had known better then I would have done better.

Let that be your mantra. As you learn from your mistakes, evolve, and realize more of your innate perfection, you will create more beautiful experiences, heal, and fall more and more in Love with your life.

One of the first steps in the learning process is also taking responsibility for how your thoughts, feelings, and actions play out in relationships, which will help you to see how the people in your life can be mirrors to broaden your awareness and help you evolve. When you account for your feelings, instead of playing the blame and shame game, you are creating a relationship and a life that is based on ultimate freedom.

"The Work"

"The Work" by Byron Katie is an absolutely fascinating tool to help you achieve forgiveness and acceptance in these uncomfortable situations. It is a system of inquiry that teaches how to turn your mind around and realize that your part in a situation may be more than what you initially see. The method reveals the multiple perspectives of a situation, which then helps to open the heart.

I would highly recommend taking the time to shift your perspective through "The Work." It takes very little to start thinking of life events in an entirely different light, and makes forgiveness that would have previously seemed miraculous, turn into the downright logical.

Death and Grief

There may be times in your life when you get hurt, really hurt, and it's difficult to imagine feeling good again. I have experienced this with grief. Only with a little more knowledge about what to expect and what intentions to have for yourself when grief occurs, you will allow yourself to feel good again sooner rather than later.

I felt the most grief of my life when my dad passed away. I took it *really* hard, and I grieved a very long time. Days, weeks, months passed, and I would still allow myself to break down in tears and have extreme emotional reactions as I went up and down the emotional ladder.

Now I realize that extending grief for so long was unnecessary. Hindsight is 20/20, and the emotional turbulence I was going through ended up hurting other areas of my life as well. It affected my job, my relationships, and my quality of life in general.

My cousin, who lost his father several years after mine, wisely said to me, "One death shouldn't take two lives." And yet, looking back, for me, it nearly did. I grieved too damn long and my woe-is-me attitude lowered the energy of my attractor field. I was attracting things and people that I did not want into my life, and yet was too unhappy for too long to do anything about it.

For instance, before this time period, I had never had any conflicts with anyone ever in line at a grocery store. And yet, early on, in my grieving process, I did! The low vibration I was walking around in brought a lady who matched it right to me. And although she appeared to be angry for other reasons, I was shocked and ashamed that I had tangoed with her.

So the beautiful tidbit I have to offer you as a result of this mismatched paradigm of a life is to let yourself grieve, but try to cap it at two weeks. Yes, two weeks, and then move on. This may seem heartless to some, but trust me, having "lived" with grief for years, what I'm telling you is *heartful*. When you reclaim your life and enjoy it, you are living the life that your deceased loved ones would want for you. It's also what your truest self wants for you.

In the play, A Death in The Family, there's a line,

"It's a kind of test Mary, and it's the only kind that amounts to anything. When something like this happens, then you have your choice. You start to really be alive, or you start to die..."

Remember this quote when something heartbreaking happens. Accept the heartbreak and move forward. These are two of the keys to it. We are all here to achieve great things in this world, and the best way to do that is by living in higher and higher energy fields. Grieving for too long can hinder that.

This is not to discount grieving. The reason we need to grieve at first, and why we feel so much like doing it is because when someone close to us passes into the next dimension there is an energetic unraveling that takes place. When my dad passed, I kept thinking to myself, 'I'm falling apart. I'm really falling apart.' Well, unbeknownst to me, at the time, I literally was.

This is because when a person passes, and they no longer exist in all the same dimensions as you, the energetic cords between you and them are un-raveled. It is almost like the stitching between two dolls comes undone. The stronger the bond was, the more there is to unravel.

Only, crying heals. This is part of the reason why we feel like doing it in the first place. And that healing can help us pull it back together. Tears are also very healing in that they help dispel negative beliefs. Have you ever had a good meltdown, and then what was bothering you before no longer seemed so important? Well, the above reasons are why I *absolutely* recommend crying your little heart out *for two*

160

weeks, and then moving on. Those two weeks will give you time to heal, and then you can get back to really living.

Additionally, if you really want to help your loved one, during and after the grieving process, try remembering them. People can take 3 months to transition into spirit, and energy helps them to make that transition. It took about that long for my dad to shift. I wanted to connect with him immediately because I felt so lost, only he was described to be cocooned up somewhere with friends, relatives and angels until he healed, and his thoughts shifted. When he finally came into his own in his spirit reality, he was able to tune down, I was able to tune up, and I started to hear from him a lot more. So if you don't hear from your loved one immediately when they pass, you'll understand why. Just give them time to gather strength and get adjusted.

In the meantime, think and speak about them as much as you can. Relive the good and the bad memories because it's all energy.

The last thing that can help you move past the grieving process is realizing that part of your grief when someone passes is actually for yourself. Intuitively, you know that they now have it way easier than you do. And you cry because you're still here on Earth, while they have moved on to a much more expanded state, and their death reminds you of the limitations that you have placed on yourself. Once you realize this, you can take action to feel good, rather than feeling sorry for yourself.

Connecting with Your Loved Ones after Death

Now I hear from my dad often. Meditation is key for this because it raises my vibration closer to his. Also being in nature, contemplating; everything we talked about in Part One. So, if you're missing your friend, family member, coworker, really anyone who has passed over, try reaching for them in your meditation or deep in contemplation. That feeling of loss and mistaken belief that you won't be able to communicate with your loved one anymore is not true. They're available to nearly anyone, anytime, anywhere. It's simply a matter of meeting them halfway.

You see, when you're deep in meditation or sleep, you're at a higher frequency, which is closer to that of their dimension. And in a more compatible vibration, you are more receptive to their messages. It is almost like being a radio and flipping up to the station where they are speaking. It might take some practice if you're not habituated to meditating, but it will happen.

How you start receiving their messages depends on what sense you tune into at the highest frequency. You could get a feeling, an image, a sound...Ask for your spirit helpers to assist you in receiving them. And if you're concerned for your loved one, ask to be given signs of their well-being. Believe me, this works. Your angels and guides will jump through hoops to help you.

Of course, you can also ask for a message from your spirit person while you sleep. My mom has not gotten much into meditating yet, and still, just the other day had a visit from her sister while she was napping. She called me absolutely amazed and grateful for the experience. In fact, it was so profound that she told me she found herself sobbing afterwards. This amazed me because I can't even count on one hand how many times I've seen her cry.

My dad is really great at visiting me in sleep as well. He's appeared to me so many times already in my dreams with messages to let me know that he is looking out for me. And just like when he was in his body, he loves to give me words of guidance. One time when he came through in a dream, we had a conversation that I cannot remember, but at the end, he said, "Good luck at your soccer game tomorrow." I was surprised when I realized that he was coming to them. So, I asked incredulously, "You come to my soccer games?" And he said, "Yes, only this is adult soccer." When I woke up, I wondered at his last comment. Then I realized that I hadn't been playing as well as I could have, and this was his way of casting some light on it.

Not every dream about a loved one is a visitation, however. Sometimes we are just working out our feelings in our sleep. You'll know when it's a real visitation, and not just a dream because you will feel the power and the love in it. You also might wake up feeling like they're still alive, and with you; like you could find them if you just walked down the hall because this is their way of telling you that they are. Their souls are forever. It is just the bodies that are finished.

Nevertheless, if you feel like you want more of a message than you are getting, or do not feel like taking the time out to get tuned up to the spirit level, then consult the help of a well-qualified medium. They can work wonders in bringing about some much needed peace in the wake of someone's passing.

Neutralizing Emotions

You may not realize it, but often you feel a certain way because you've been conditioned to believe that you must feel that way. Realizing this can help you to raise your vibration out of any negative emotion. This idea of neutralizing emotions comes from Bashar. The way it works is simply through bringing awareness to the real reason why you're feeling them. When you state to yourself that you're feeling a certain way because basically you've been conditioned to it, it brings your negative beliefs to light, and helps you to overcome the conditioning.

Neutralizing Emotions

When you become aware that you're feeling a certain way, and you want to step out of it, or draw awareness to it, say to yourself,

"I feel _____ because I believe that I have to."

It is important to state this when you are not only feeling badly, but feeling good as well because it takes acknowledging both sides of the coin to realize how very much our belief systems are influencing how we react to different circumstances.

Suicide and the Death Penalty

I can't broach the subject of death without also sharing some insights on suicide. What's worth noting is that people generally choose suicide they are unaware of the numerous other possibilities that lie before them. It is almost like they are walking down a long hallway with many doors, but they only see the one at the end. In other words, they aren't conscious of any other way of getting back to their true self. They feel powerless, which is almost completely opposite what we naturally feel, and this leads to a state of mind in which it is easy to entertain suicide: the only presumed way of taking back their power.

Why is it important to address this issue? Because one day you might find yourself contemplating it. It's easy to do in the valleys of life. I've done it myself. Only if you recall that all roads lead to Rome, and step by step you can make it back to who you are, then you will be more likely to take a clear look around for the other doors before you choose to step out on life.

It may take courage to take another path, only that reaching will create a better feeling, a feeling that leans towards hope, and hope can be your guidepost to an even higher energy. Moreover, you'll see that you can continue giving and receiving on this planet, even if at times it's from a lower emotional vibration. You may even transcend to what the challenges are teaching you, which in hard times can be tough to do.

It is also crucial to remember when you're inching closer to the ledge to go back to the intent of loving yourself. Just setting the intention will at least be a distraction from your problems if not leading to other avenues. And when you get to loving yourself more, you'll be less likely to harm your body which would be quite the contradiction for someone of a non-violent, peaceful, self-loving nature.

On the other hand, is the judgment surrounding suicide really justified? It sucks when it happens. Only we all have free will; and what is self-termination, but another decision; a decision to leave the body, which in reality doesn't even end life, but simply changes its form. Looking at it from an unbiased perspective, the person committing it isn't getting what they want here, so they're gonna give it a go in another dimension.

It's the people who are left on Earth who suffer the most of course. I would initially be very upset if someone I loved left purposefully, however, I would have to remember that they made their decision freely, and now, please forgive the cliché, but they're in a much better place.

The fact that people have it a lot better when they leave their bodies is the primary reason, I don't believe in the death penalty. Yes, people put to death have made some pretty horrifying decisions, however, sending them on to expansion and bliss is hardly a punishment. They're much better off learning and reaping their karma in jail here on Earth than being given an escape route. The channel, Abraham-Hicks said quite enlighteningly, "If we knew where they were going, we wouldn't kill them."

I was actually reading about someone being put to death as family members of his victim looked on. Much to their dismay, as the man was slipping into the next dimension; he was also expressing his awe and appreciation of it. Perhaps in the larger scheme, he was shown his heaven in such a public way as a means of drawing awareness to the *actual* result of the death penalty.

And so, it is with our loved ones' passing and suicides. It is tragic for those of us left behind, only we have to see that they are happier and healthier. They made what they believed was the best choice for them at the time.

Your Highest Excitement

Only to live so well that we delay death as long as possible, we need to make the most of the life we have. One of the keys to that is to follow your highest excitement. Whenever I focus my energies on this intent, amazing things happen, and life is a gift once again.

The channeled being, Bashar, emphasizes this idea. He teaches that in every moment make choices that will allow you to live with the most enthusiasm, *without* having any expectations of the results.

This is not always an easy choice because of the conditioning in which we've been brought up. However, we can't let that be an excuse. Instead, we can model it, teach it to our children, and let our wave and that of the next generation living in their highest excitements change the world.

My mom is an example of one of the baby boomers who models this. She lives in a retirement community that she swears is like a summer camp. I initially begged her not to live there because I imagined a world where older people were dying off. Instead, it's a world where elder people are living life to its fullest. They've raised their kids. They've had their careers. Now they just want to make the most of the time they have left.

I've found athletes who play extreme sports exemplify this too. No one is forcing their hand to participate in these semi-dangerous activities. They often aren't paid, nor is it expected of them. They're in it for the fun of it, and I get it because I love Kiteboarding. You're flying with the wind, having an adrenaline filled adventure, and you *have* to be present. Those kinds of activities are perfect for me.

Nonetheless, your highest excitement could be as simple as cooking, watching a movie, studying, or doing some research on something you just heard about. It could be anything! The point is just giving yourself the ultimate freedom regardless of what other people are doing around you to do what you feel in the moment is intuitively the best thing for you. So, trust your intuition. Your gut feelings will lead you to the next and then the next and the next best things. And as you follow through consistently, eventually you'll find yourself with more and more people who are also making intuitive choices.

And believe it or not, when you live your highest joy in the moment, you will actually accomplish a lot more. You can do multiple times the amount of things living from moment to moment in joy and excitement than you would doing dull things that you really don't enjoy. And this is because we don't live linearly. When we jump to higher wavelengths, we also jump to higher energy choices.

Example: have you ever noticed that when you're doing something that you don't really want to be doing that you get tired more quickly? Well, who wouldn't want to go to sleep in a tired slowed down wavelength? At least if you do, you can start over when you wake up.

Living this way is not the linear path you have been taught to expect, but it will improve your quality of life.

Here is the reasoning behind this:

1. Time speeds up when we're having fun. (We've all experienced it.)
2. When you release expectations, and judgments; you're open to more diverse avenues that will give you the same or better results, including the miraculous.
3. When you are happily living in the moment, you are actually already living the life you came here to live.

So just ask yourself when you're worrying or stuck in negative thinking, "Is this what is bringing me the most excitement and joy in my life right now?" Just calling it out can be the reset button that will pull you out. It will bring you back to the present moment and give you the permission to stop doing what you really don't want to be doing and start really living.

Sometimes being in your highest excitement can be as simple as coming back to the present; directing yourself to stop running around in your head and just appreciate. This creates some incredible enjoyable, life-giving experiences. For me, there are moments when I'm playing soccer where I feel completely present. Running after the ball sometimes, it is like it's the only thing that exists. It's bliss. No wonder my dog and I get along so well.

Emotional Healing

It can be difficult to remain present and choose your highest excitement because you might need some serious emotional healing. The year following my father's death was an emotional roller coaster. And then, the year after that, my relationship ended with the man I wanted to marry, and I was a wreck. My thoughts were taking me down dark rabbit holes, and I could see things were getting out of hand.

So I went to the channeling at my Metaphysical church see if they could help me. The response changed my life profoundly. The first thing said was that I had a holy aura. I of course took this as a compliment. And then they spelled it out for me, not H-O-L-Y, but H-O-L-E-Y. 'Hmmm,' I thought. 'Not as complimentary as I thought. But what is a holey aura?'

Come to find out, a holey aura is one with a lot of holes as a result of traumatic experiences. To say I did not take my father nor my lover leaving well would be a gross understatement, so I could only imagine the size of the holes those trials had rent.

When a person has enough of these holes, energy moves swiftly in and out their energy field, which causes quick emotional upsets. It can happen to anyone. So, if you find yourself crying at commercials or getting really angry at the smallest slight, chances are, you may have some holes in your aura too. This next exercise will help you to heal them.

The Cocoon

To heal the holes, I was instructed to do a powerful visualization that I like to call the "The Cocoon." It works wonders.

The Cocoon

Imagine wrapping your aura with a long strip of white light around and around, similar to how you would wrap a mummy with a long strip of white cloth.

The light is programmed by you to seal any holes.

Remember your aura is egg shaped and extends 2-3 feet out from your physical body.

Start by doing this every day for a week, and then move on to every other day for another couple weeks or so until you've achieved consistent emotional stability...

Revisit this visualization when you notice any unnecessary emotional turbulence or following trauma.

Once you start practicing this visualization, a renewed sense of calm will come over you. It will bring you back to your natural state. Within hours and days, your life will improve, and you'll come back to a fuller, calmer version of you.

I am so grateful to have come by this practice that even now, years later, if I come into contact with someone with a similar problem, I share this technique with them.

Healing Excessive Emotionality with Water

Another piece of advice I received then that also helped significantly was to sit by a body of water. When you're close to a large amount of water you will exchange energy with it, which in turn balances emotions. So when I was upset, I would just ride my bike to the closest pond and relax.

Further, in order to make the most of the current of energy flowing into and out of you, try blessing the water with love before and as it flows into you. The water will leave you feeling calmer and more balanced.

If you've ever spent the day at the beach, you can attest to that. This is also partly because of the cleansing saltwater and negative ions. If you are unable to bathe in the ocean, however, have a salt bath, and pretend it is the ocean. This is also effective. If you do not have a bathtub, try turning off the shower, rubbing your body down with salt, standing for a few minutes while the salt cleanses your energy field. (You can imagine it lifting out of your aura.) And then rinse it off.

Homeopathic baths are also very healing for many different energetic issues. There are instructions for many of them in the book, *Spiritual Cleansing* by Draja Mickaharic.

Color baths can also do wonders. Depending on the problems you're facing, add the appropriate color to your bath. This will in turn add more of that color's frequency to your energy field. For example, if you're feeling out of sorts, a blue bath will increase that color and the comforting energy it brings to your aura.

Healing Excessive Emotionality with Water

- *Spend time by bodies of water.*
- *Take salt baths and showers.*
- *Take homeopathic baths, including color baths.*

Spiritual Help with Sleeping

There are few things that can help a person more when they're going through a challenging time than the renewing power of sleep. Only when you're experiencing unrest sleep can be difficult to achieve. Try some of these techniques to help you get a good, consistent night's sleep.

If you ever feel alone, although in truth, we are never alone, when you are getting ready to go to sleep, imagine an angel wrapping its arms around you; engulfing you with its "wings" of love. This could be your guardian angel, an archangel, or any loving angel. Its reassuring presence will set you at ease.

Additionally, if you are stirred up over something, ask for 1000s of calming, comforting angels to help you to calm down and sleep. They'll work similarly, though you may not feel the wrapped wings.

Another easy thing to do to help you fall asleep is to distract yourself from the problem you're facing you. I know it seems pretty standard, but sometimes it helps to be reminded. I used to wake up in the middle of the night and try to solve my problems. Now, I rarely do this. Instead, I'll meditate, sometimes with YouTube, or write. Naturally, when the mind is entrained in something pleasant, it's easier to relax and fall sleep.

The final thing that I discovered which really helped me to sleep was to channel energy to myself. The love vibration will put you right to sleep if you let it. I would also recommend using the position of self-love for this exercise. This adds to the comfort of the energy channeled, and you will be much more likely to awaken peacefully and blissfully.

If you're also tempted like I was to solve problems at inopportune times for sleep, there is another important time to reflect and receive, and that is when you're just waking up. In that in between state where you are still super receptive, yet almost awake enough to remember, tune yourself to an awareness where you will remember, and ask for some insight. Then as you come out of it, write it down immediately. It can be a supreme meditation

Enjoy this process, and when you get a message that really helps your life, be grateful. That energy will help keep the great messages coming, and let the good times roll!

Channeling Energy to Yourself for Sleep

Turn your light on to Source and program it for peace and love.

Then cross your arms, and put your hands on the middle of each arm, and then channel that energy in through your head, heart, hands, and into your body again.

With intention, fill yourself with the Love of Source. Know that you are very, very loved. Enjoy a good night's sleep.

Tricks to Help You Sleep in an Emotional Time

Ask to be wrapped in the arms of an angel.

Ask for 1000s of calming comforting angels to comfort you.

Read something pleasant.

Play high vibrational music.

Allow yourself to be talked into sleep through a guided meditation.

Channel energy to yourself.

PART FOUR

MANIFESTATION

"Learn to be thankful for what you already have while you pursue all that you want." -Jim Rohn

Intuition

Initially I didn't really understand how easy following your intuition can be. In spite of knowing it exists, I was still terrified of making bad choices, so terrified in fact, that for a period of time, I would do nothing without consulting my pendulum.

This method of inquiry was fun, and I felt eager to do it. However, one has to be careful not to develop a dependency on it. (I would even take mine out in restaurants when I was deciding what to order, much to the amusement of my friends.)

If you would like to start using a pendulum (I recommend in moderation.), all it takes is saying a prayer of protection, and asking a question. Yes/No questions are relatively easy once you know which direction the pendulum goes for yes and for no. You can determine that first by asking. Additionally, if you have a lot of choices, you can draw out a diagram of all of them. Then ask which one is for the highest good. The pendulum will swing to the correct one.

My dependency stemmed from the thinking that if something was for the highest good, then each choice would have effects going out that would be far beyond my reach, so how could I, a mere mortal, know which was best? The pendulum was always best.

Well, eventually consulting my pendulum became a little much. It was time consuming, and I got tired of using a tool for everything. Even though I thought I felt more comfortable with the choices I was making, it was slowing me down. I also could see that my lower self rather than my higher self was sometimes unconsciously influencing the pendulum. So it seemed reasonable that I transition into making more of my own choices without using it. Finally, but how would I still feel comfortable with my decisions and not be paralyzed by fear?

And then it dawned on me. Why don't I just do whatever I *feel* like doing? This may be obvious to some, but I was a little slow in the arena of trusting my gut instincts. I had a tool, and I wanted to use it. If feelings are actually the way that I guide me at a Higher Level, then that would make a lot more sense. Granted, sometimes it takes a bit of relaxation to get in touch with my feelings; it would still take less effort than I was putting into drawing up the choice charts, speaking my pendulum protection prayer, and waiting for it to move.

Since learning to rely on my feelings, I've had some interesting experiences with it. On my birthday a couple of years ago, I went on a boat ride with my boyfriend and a few other friends off the coast of Maui. First, we went to a well known spot to snorkel, and then the captain took us to a little known spot. There, my boyfriend and I got out of the boat, and swam in one direction, and our friends got out, and swam the other way. After about 5 minutes of swimming, I got an eerie feeling. I felt like I needed to get back to the boat right that moment. I rationalized it with the thought that maybe my boyfriend was tired, and needed a rest, so I motioned to him that I wanted to go back, and within a short while we were on the boat again.

It wasn't too long after we had boarded, however, that we heard the shout, "Shark!" Our other friends swimming had spotted a huge shark and wanted us to come pick them up by boat. One was an experienced snorkeler, and he wanted to stay there and keep an eye on it, rather than attempting to swim back. The other was new to Maui and could barely swim. We headed over to them, and thankfully they boarded fine. I was just so terribly grateful that they were safe, that I was not in the water when I heard the shout, and also that I didn't spot one myself because I was not prepared for that. Moral of the story: trust your gut.

Now let me give you an example of something equally valid that happened as a result of listening to my feelings. Recently, while on a trip to Southern Baja, I heard that people there swim with the whale sharks. I looked them up and found out that whale sharks are the largest fish in the ocean. They have no teeth, move slowly, and are relatively harmless. They're just very big, and they look like sharks. I was super excited about being so close to them, so I got two other couples to hire a guide boat with us, and the next morning we all rode out into the Sea of Cortez. Even though I still had some inhibitions about jumping into the water with a shark, I did it anyway, and it was some of the best snorkeling of my life. The sense of wonder on and off that boat was palpable. Swimming with an underwater beast that large is like a dream brought to life.

So, there you have it. If you feel like doing something, then do it! Feel the magic! And when you feel like getting out of the water, get out! Don't waste your time thinking about it. Just do it! Trust your instincts because our higher selves that control our intuition do see farther than us. One of the best metaphors I've heard is our Earthly Selves are walking along the road of life; wondering whether we should make the next turn, and our Higher Selves are above us looking at the whole map! That's how they know where to turn, and where the next one will lead, and the next, and so on, and so forth.

And, since they are a part of us, they naturally want what is best for us, so it is wise and wonderful to listen to and trust our higher selves and let them be our guides. And you don't need a pendulum to do it, although it can be helpful when you're lacking clarity on which doctor or lawyer to call out of the phone book. We naturally know what's best for us, so trust your feelings and vibes because it really is a wise and wonderful You who is guiding you.

Pendulum Protection Prayer

Anytime you do spiritual work, say a prayer of protection prayer. This is especially handy when you're using a pendulum or consulting cards, i.e. Tarot.

Example:

"To my Higher Self, Guardian Angels, and Sprit Guides: I ask your protection as I do this work. Surround and protect me with white light. Do not allow any harm to come to me or to others. Do not allow me to be negatively influenced as I do this work. May the information that I receive be 100% accurate and may it be used for the best and highest good of all.

With Thanks and In Full Faith. So be it."
-Source Unknown

Spirit Guides

Spirit Guides are spiritual beings assigned to us before birth to help us navigate the waters of Earth. I initially learned about them through Sylvia Brown's books, and they immediately ignited a spark of wonder in me. According to Sylvia, Spirit Guides are like invisible friends who guide us throughout our life.

Since I came from a relatively religious upbringing this was all new to me, and I was very curious. 'Who are they?' I wondered. 'What are their names? How are they guiding me?' "Spirit Guide, give me a sign," I would say. Initially, I would hear very little which is pretty much what they sound like in our dimension. Until that is, I went into meditation, and did some exploring with them. Then, I got some results: words that were like whispers and visions that fleeted so quickly that sometimes I wondered what I had just seen...They seemed very benevolent though. So, I kept at it...

Let me give you the lowdown on what I do know about Spirit Guides. There are five, and they each have specific duties. There is the Master Guide, the Native American Guide, the Doctor-Healer, the Doctor-Teacher, and the Joy Guide. The Master Guide is the principal one, your main squeeze, the Native American is helpful with trail blazing, the doctor-Healer heals, and the Doctor Teacher teaches of course, and the Joy Guide helps you to connect with just that. It's simple, right?

So, how do you help them help you? Well, first just acknowledge them and incorporate them into your day-to-day life. Like when I was reading a book that I was confused by, I asked my doctor-teacher to help me assimilate the best knowledge from it seamlessly. I would also explore with each one in meditation and see what messages you get. They all have different personalities, and they all have different gifts, so it is helpful to consult with each of them.

There is also the idea floating around that our Spirit Guides are all different aspects of us. In other words, we are all consciously in one body; connected to a Soul through our Higher Selves, and our current self has these helpers that come from within to create with us on our journeys. It's still a fantastic possibility, and yet now we have no one to blame for our choices but ourselves.

Speaking of Guides in Spirit, Doreen Virtue has an excellent book that explains the importance and uniqueness of the different ascended masters and archangels. You may want to check it out when you're looking for spiritual help and guidance. It's called *Archangels and Ascended Masters*.

Opening to Different Forms of Abundance and Vibration

Now that you have an idea of the juicy ideas you can turn to for spiritual guidance and healing, here are some tools for getting what you want in the material realm. According to Lynne Twist in her book, *The Soul of Money,* one of the major keys to this, is to let go of the belief in the lie of scarcity and embrace instead the truth of sufficiency. This first paradigm shift will indeed help energy to flow in abundance.

Additionally, we need to release the limits in our thinking on how we can acquire abundance. The first thing that usually comes to mind when you think about abundance is money. Only you don't actually always need money to acquire what you want. In fact, it is only one avenue among many. So be careful about putting money as a limit to getting something because when you do you are limiting all the other ways in which it could come to you.

When you truly realize this, you'll allow all the rivers of abundance to flow, not just the money one. For example, passage to Hawaii can be bought. However, it can also be gifted. You could be a flight attendant, find space on a ship delivering goods or get a job on a Hawaiian cruise line...These are just a few of the million ways that you could make it to Hawaii if you really wanted to. Only one of which involves buying a ticket. So, when you want something, please don't make money the limiting factor.

I personally love flying, and the last time I flew, the airline asked me to bump my flight back. When I agreed, they gave me $1500 in travel credits. Abundance speaks loudly. I was in tears.

There is also a process of thinking that can lead you to opening up to receiving what you really want. For some, this might already come naturally. Nevertheless, here are a few questions to ask yourself with your intention in mind when you are creating.

First, especially if you're feeling stuck, try asking yourself, "What is the next right thing to do?" And then doing whatever you feel the answer is, even if it seems silly. If more people gave themselves this freedom on a day-to-day basis, the world would be a happier place.

The second question is to be asked when you would like to do something that seems very difficult: "What would it take for me to?"

Although the answers may not immediately pop out of the sky and land on your lap, Source will provide them, and you will respond in one way or another because you can't help but shift with them. This question will also help keep your emotional body more hopeful, which will allow you to be in even more of a state of allowing.

A third question to ask on a regular basis when you are in the process of achieving a state of abundance is: "Am I feeling good?" Because if you're not, something has got to change so that you can match the frequency of who you want to be more easily. It will also help you to tune up to the answers of the previous questions.

The reason you want to feel good is that positive emotions are indicators from your Higher Self that you are on the right track. Not feeling good is a sign for life to change. And life can be so enjoyable when you're constantly, consciously focused on making yourself happy.

Also, choosing to feel good and be happy can also help others by just being a vibrational example in their vicinity. Regardless of what they decide though, just keep doing what you do. And in already being happy for what you have, you'll attract more of what you want.

Three Questions to Ask Yourself to Achieve Abundance

1. *What is the next right thing to do?*
2. *What would it take for me to…?*
3. *Am I feeling good?*

Gratitude

You can get yourself out of some tough places through the power of gratitude. For instance, after my most painful break-up, I actually told my spiritual teacher that I hated my life. (Anger and hate are only a few steps up from depression on the emotional ladder though, so I guess I was on the right track in coming back up.) She responded that I should focus on what I'm grateful for, and then I would learn to love my life.

So, in a desperate attempt to make myself feel better, I decided to try a tool that Oprah had advocated on TV many years before:

"Make a list of the ten things you are grateful for every night before going to sleep in a gratitude journal."

I started the practice, and after only a short time of documenting all my blessings in my life, of which there were actually many (I had been ignoring them), my emotions improved, and my life took a sharp turn for the better. In fact, it was so effective that I am still writing down my lists. When you're already grateful for what you have, you're more likely to let more in. It's a cycle of abundance.

I also know a lady who did the Oprah gratitude practice with a twist. Every evening she would make her gratitude list, and then she would add one thing that she wanted. She did this over and over and over again.

One day I saw her, and I commented that she wasn't wearing glasses anymore. Happily, and a little shyly she explained her gratitude practice to me. The last item that was often on her list: perfect vision. No Lasik or contacts for her; just gratitude! I was amazed. She literally had performed a miracle.

And so, there it is. One of the keys to abundance: You get what you want when you love what you have.

Vision Boards

Visualizing is an amazing tool for creating what you want. Try it! Spend 2-3 minutes now actively visualizing yourself somewhere, and I mean in detail. Then don't be surprised when one day, and it could be soon, that you actually find yourself there. I did this several years ago when I hadn't taken a trip in a while. I imagined myself on an airplane, and damn if I wasn't on one within a couple of months. It had been years since I had been on one! I also had my goddaughter do that when I wanted her to visit. I had her see a plane ticket with her name on it. She's flown from Florida to California a few times and once to Hawaii. She's only 16.

I had another incredible experience after listening to a guided meditation on YouTube. I was instructed to imagine myself running at the head of a pack of wolves. It was exhilarating! I'd never done it before, and it felt amazing to be at the head of that pack. Well, within a month, I found myself running on a beach in Mexico, at the head of a pack of loving, friendly German Shepherds feeling that same rush.

Visualizing can be made even easier through the use of vision boards. Vision boards are effective because they focus and stimulate the imagination. And the imagination is where all the manifesting magic happens. Creating a vision board is super easy. All it takes is cutting images and words of things you would like to create out of magazines, newspapers, etc. and pasting the pictures in a place where you'll see them often.

I made one in particular of beautiful beach scenes when I still lived in Jacksonville. A year later, I was moving to Hawaii. Coincidence? I don't think so.

With visualizing, you end up with a reality often more splendid than the one you began with. It helps dreams come true, and it all starts in your mind.

The Three Ohms

The following is a tool that uses the power of visualization along with the power of sound to raise your vibration and create the blessings you want in your life. My friend, Ryan, who lives in Hawaii, reminded me of it when I moved here the first time. It works because the word, "Ohm" is of a cosmic vibration. Some say it is even the name of God.

The tool is of two parts: visualization and chanting. The visualizing will bring the vibration of what you want into your energy field which makes it that much closer to allowing it in your physicality. While the toning automatically elevates you up towards the abundant you that you're creating. Ryan and I practiced this together. We had some fun and satisfying results.

The Three Ohms

Visualize wholeheartedly. Feel it, taste it, see it, hear it, live it.

Chant three Ohms with the vision in mind.

Affirmations

Affirmations are a great way of tuning your vibration to what you want, which will then bring it in because they help to redefine your beliefs to align with the healthy, positive self you're stepping into.

It goes to recognize how powerful our words are, especially when we voice them. Take the Hawaiian greeting, "Aloha" for example. It means hello and goodbye as well as love, compassion, respect, and affection. If you visit Hawaii, you'll notice that in hearing and saying "Aloha" has a calming effect on the nervous system. And the more emotion there is in its vocalization, the more powerful it can be. This just one word though. As you string them together, you can either uplift or you can tear down.

Affirmations can even create new beliefs because if you tell yourself something enough, and by that, I mean even just a couple hundred times, you will create a belief. And as you may know, beliefs are very, very influential because they shape our lives.

This is good to know because if you believe that something is good for you, you will choose it. That's just how humans behave. We look out for what we perceive as our best interests. Healthier beliefs will therefore help you to make better choices. It's ultimately up to you though to decide which beliefs are harmful and replace them with ones that help.

Affirmations will also assist you in having more mental flexible , which will also help you as you reformat your belief system. Additionally, as you replace outdated thinking by choosing affirmations of higher and higher vibrations, you are getting closer to the truth of who you truly are.

Just don't forget that the fuel to the fire of affirmations is the emotion you put behind them. So you may choose to affirm them when you're already in a good mood. Then they will be easier to affirm them later when you aren't feeling as good because you'll be stepping into an already practiced vibration.

That way even if you don't resonate with what you're saying, you can still act the part until you are the part. "Fake it 'til you make it" they say. Well, say it like you mean it, and that emotion, that energy is going to change your mind, create new beliefs, and transform your life.

There are also certain phrases to begin your affirmations that will make them more powerful, and those are, "I am," which also translates into the name of God, and "I have."

One affirmation that is particularly powerful in terms of manifestation is "I am so happy and grateful for..." Say it at least twice. The first time fill it in with what you already have in your life. And then when your vibration has shifted to one of gratitude, fill it in with what you want in your life. For example, say, you have a puppy and yet you want peace. You would first say, "I am so happy and grateful for my puppy," and then "I am so happy and grateful for peace" with equal if not greater conviction. Essentially the second affirmation is piggybacking on the energy of the first, and it may take some practice to bring you up to resonance.

Always remember though when you're experimenting with different ways to raise your frequency that anyone can be grateful for something after the fact. It is the master who is grateful beforehand. Let that be your rationale as you move through any doubt.

Another powerful affirmation for changing thought paradigms and allowing more of what you want into your life is "I have the freedom to..." whatever you most want to do...

I recently affirmed, "I have the freedom to get free massages." And in the coming weekend, I received two free massages, one without me even asking for it. It was quite wonderful. (I also recommend adding,

"No strings attached" so that although the circle of energy will be complete, it will be up to you and/or the cosmic forces of the universe how and where that energy is returned.)

One of my favorite affirmations of all time is from Kanye West. When he was just getting started, the comedian, Dave Chappelle quoted him as saying, "I am dope, and my life is dope." Well, you see where believing this truth has brought him. I may not agree with everything he has done, but I do agree that he has achieved a measure of success.

Another affirmation that can help you to feel right about where you are and help you to create the best circumstances in your life is to say,

"I am doing the right and correct thing at the right and correct time."

I have a sticky note with this written on my mirror. It is one of the affirmations I read as I am getting ready. Personally, it reassures me. It gives me greater confidence and I feel more secure.. It has also helped me to snap out of making choices that do not bring me joy, and are therefore not who I truly am.

I can remember times in my life where I have been doing one thing and wondering if it would have been better to have made another choice, and this affirmation shakes all that loose. It grounds and balances. Saying it helps you come back to the moment.

Now let's move on to a trick to help you not only to activate your imagination, but also open you up to the impossible. It harnesses the energy of the moon and the Earth.

Moon Manifestations

Let me begin by explaining that Moon Manifestations are very, very powerful. They originated off planet and doing one can be fun. All it requires is asking for several things in great detail, and then following a few simple steps according to the phases of the moon.

I believe in this process because I have received A LOT through my moon manifestations: new, jobs, beautiful clothes, a car, vacations, new friends, boyfriends...Even several years ago, I heard that we create our own salaries, so, in my moon manifestation, I set my salary at time and a half of what I was making at my last job, and sure enough, when I switched jobs that was my salary.

Moon Manifestations

*On the day, or even better, at the exact time of the New Moon, write down 7 things that you want to manifest, in detail. ***

Study your list as much as you like during the next two weeks. Visualizing helps.

Then on the day, or even time of the next Full Moon, burn your list; putting the ashes either directly into living, running water like a river or stream; or burying them in the Earth.

*Emphasis is on in detail because you could ask for a guitar, and later on someone hands you an electric when what wanted was an acoustic. It'd be glorious, but disappointing, so be specific! Also, for either or both of these processes, it is even more helpful if you do them in ceremony.

"Ask and you shall receive."

Try harnessing the energies of our Earth and Moon in this fashion and watch the magic happen.

A New Generation and How to Be a Part of It

There is a new generation of children being born who are more intuitive, empathic, and telepathic. They're known as the indigo, crystal and star children. You may have heard of them, you may have one as a child, or you may even be one. They are different and bring a new energy to the Earth. The indigos have come first, and are effectively the placeholders for the others, here to usher in the new and different energies of the crystal and Starseeds.

The indigos are important because in a major shift, like the one we are in now, the Earth cannot go directly from one spectrum of light beings to another without there being an upset. There has to be a middle spectrum in between, and that is where the indigos come in.

It is not the easiest thing in the world to be an indigo, particularly not an indigo teenager. They don't fit in in the old world, and the new world hasn't completely happened yet. They never feel quite like they belong. Only these indigos, however sensitive, are also strong and resilient. They have survived, we have survived, and our energy has ushered and continues to usher in the star and the crystal generations.

I feel like understanding why this indigo generation exists is helpful to our evolution. People in our society have a strong proclivity for blaming their parents for what they did or did not do. However, once you understand that that generation was of an entirely different energy, it's easier to be more understanding of their "mis-takes." You can stop looking into the past for the answers, and instead focus on creating them.

This is what we special people are doing as we grow up. We're also starting to take a greater part in the world, and the world is changing with us. Soon, for instance, telepathy, which is now only mentioned here and there, will be commonplace.

My brother is one such individual. He's grown now, and not into metaphysics at all, and yet he is very sensitive. Even on the phone, I am sometimes saying one thing, only my energy reads something else that I haven't yet even put it into a thought form, and he will call me out on it. It is very funny. I was telling someone about it, and they said we have this connection because we are siblings, and yet I have seen my brother do the same thing with others unrelated to us. He has a gift. It comes from being super-intuitive and of the next generation of energy.

I also used to nanny for a very young child who was telepathic. She was nearly two, and I would place 3 crayons in front of her, and then "shine the color" of the crayon I wanted her to pick in her mind. More than 2 out of 3 times she would pick the correct one. Through this exercise, I like to think that I gave her a structured start in developing her telepathy, while practicing my own.

I have even worked with my partner to develop the telepathy between us. I love it when he reads my mind, so we sometimes practice when we're out to eat, and waiting for our food. I think of a word or a color and project it to him, and then him to me. We each have three tries to get it, and we usually get it within three. (I believe part of our talent though is when I was manifesting a boyfriend, I asked for a man who could share telepathy with me.)

Anyway, these are just a couple simple exercises to open your mind to the idea of telepathy. It is one of the gifts that this new energy of people are bringing with them. And although unique, it is up to us to embrace, foster, and love the newness of us, understanding that although this way is not the usual, this generation is ushering in what will be normal in the future, more love and more light.

The following channeled visualization is one that I recommend for increasing your telepathy, teleportation and telekinetic abilities. I haven't yet dived much into the latter two, but it helps with all of them.

Visualization to Increase your Telepathy, Telekinesis, and Teleportation

See 3 of the glands in your brain: your pineal, pituitary and your hippocampus. Then form a golden triangle of light between them. Then see each gland lighting up when the golden line hits it.

CONCLUSION

As you go back through this book and practice all the exercises that have resonated with you, look at it as an opportunity to grow, evolve, and step into more of who you are. I pray that *The Metaphysical Handbook* has furthered you in many ways, and that it helps usher in an era of peace, love, and understanding..

Thank you for the opportunity to pass this knowledge on.

I look forward to all the enlightenment and gifts that are to come.

ACKNOWLEDGEMENTS

I want to thank:

My teacher, Reverend Mary Cox. Thank you for all the beautiful information you channeled, and of course, thank you for the love.

Everyone at The Cosmic Church of Truth. We are all each other's teachers. I am forever grateful to this group that welcomed me with so much kindness and acceptance. *www.cosmic-church.org*

Soofeeya Tamseel for your lovely cover art.

My partner, Napoleon. You helped me manifest the perfect writing abode and you bring me so much joy. Mahalo nui loa.

SOURCES

Brennan, Barabara. Hands of Light. New York, New York. Pleaides Books, 1987.

Carroll, L, Tober, J., The Indigo Children: The New Kids Have Arrived. Carlsbad, California: Hay House: 1999.

Co, S., Robbins, E., Merryman, J. Your Hands Can Heal You: Pranic Healing Energy Remedies to Boost Vitality and Speed Recovery from Common Health Problems. New York, New York: Simon and Schuster, 2002.

Chapman, Gary. The Five Love Languages. Chicago, Illinois: Northfield Publishing, 1992.

Dyer, Wayne. Secrets of Manifesting. Carlsbad, California: Hay House, 2012.

Emoto, Masuru. The Hidden Messages in Water. New York, NY: Atria Books, 2005.

Ford, D., Chopra, D., Williamson, M. The Shadow Effect: Illuminating the Hidden Power of Your True Self. San Francisco, CA: HarperOne, 2009.

Hay, Louise. You Can Heal Your Life. Carlsbad, California: Hay House, 1984.

Katie, Byron. Loving What Is: Four Questions That Can Change Your Life. 2002.

Mickaharic, Draja. Spiritual Cleansing A Handbook of Psychic Self-Protection. San Francisco, California: Weiser Books, 2003.

Megre, Vladimir. The Space of Love. The United Kingdom: The Ringing Series Press, 2000.

Myss, Caroline. Defy Gravity: Healing Beyond the Bounds of Reason. Carlsbad, California: Hay House, 2011.

Ounes, S., Popp, J. (2019, March 1). High Cortisol and the Risk of Dementia and Alzheimer's Disease: A Review of the Literature. Retrieved from: https://www.ncbi.nlm.nih.gov/pmc/articles/PMC6405479/

Sharma, Robin. The Monk Who Sold His Ferrari. Mumbai, India: Jaico Publishing House, 2005.

Steinfield, Alan. [NewRealities]. (September 26, 2006). Bashar: Finding Your Highest Excitement Retrieved from https://www.youtube.com/watch?v=OB-NLlwzfOM

[SpiritualBuff]. (October 8, 2014). Abraham Hicks - Bad Things Happen For a Reason. Retrieved from https://www.youtube.com/watch?v=lG9-mXCw3Io

Twist, Lynne. The Soul of Money. New York, New York: W.W. Norton & Company, 2017.

Vanderlinden, Colleen. (2019, April 28). Its True-You Really Should Talk to Your Plants. Retrieved from: https://www.thespruce.com/should-you-talk-to-your-plants-3972298

[Vio77X]. (November 13, 2010). Abraham-Hicks - When is it time to move on? Retrieved from

https://www.youtube.com/watch?v=ECaT5tacN_w

Virtue, Doreen. Archangels and Ascended Masters A Guide to Working and Healing with Divinities and Deities. Carlsbad, California: Hay House, 2004.

Printed in Great Britain
by Amazon

85676701R00125